GLUTEN-FREE BAKING
FOR THE HOLIDAYS

GLUTEN-FREE BAKING FOR THE HOLIDAYS

60 RECIPES FOR TRADITIONAL FESTIVE TREATS

BY JEANNE SAUVAGE

PHOTOGRAPHS BY CLARE BARBOZA

CHRONICLE BOOKS

SAN FRANCISCO

Library of Congress Cataloging-in-Publication Data available.
ISBN 978-1-4521-0701-1

Manufactured in China

Designed by Supriya Kalidas

eBay is a registered trademark of eBay Inc.; Emile Henry is a registered trade-
mark of Emile Henry; Grand Marnier is a registered trademark of Societe des
Produits Marnier-Lapostolle; Microplane is a registered trademark of Grace
Manufacturing Co.; Pyrex is a registered trademark of Corning Inc.; Silpat
Nonstick Baking Mat is a registered trademark of ETS Guy Demarle; SunButter
is a registered trademark of Red River Commodities, Inc.

10 9 8 7 6 5 4 3 2 1

Chronicle Books LLC
680 Second Street
San Francisco, California 94107
www.chroniclebooks.com

TO KIM RICKETTS,

who left us before she could see this book.
I love you and I miss you desperately.

My deepest gratitude:

To my editor, Amy Treadwell, who believed in and took a chance on me.

To Doug Ogan, Claire Fletcher, Vanessa Dina, Tera Killip, Peter Perez, David Hawk, and the entire staff at Chronicle Books, who have made me feel so welcome.

To my agents, Lisa and Sally Ekus, and to Jaimee Constantine, who have been kind angels leading me through the wilderness of book publishing and contracts and giving me support around every turn.

To my comrade in arms and dear friend, Kim O'Donnel, who showed me the way and supported me every step of my journey. I have no words for how grateful I am to have you in my life.

To my fairy godmothers, Kim Ricketts, Myra Kohn, Stephanie Gailing, and Nicole Aloni. You believed in me since the start and have been never failing in your support and good cheer. I can't believe how lucky I am to have you in my life. Your fairy dust makes this book sparkly and pretty.

To Becca Knox, who was my original—and still best—gluten-free guide and mentor. Thank you for your wisdom, good humor, and support.

To Clare Barboza, my dream photographer, who brought these recipes to life in the most beautiful photos I could ever dare to hope for. And to Helene Dujardin, whose styling for the photos was perfection itself.

To my amazing recipe testers, in no particular order: Autumn Giles, Stacy Jensen, Joan Funk, Karen Murphy, Ginger Garza, Alice Shipman, Tammy Kirschner, Jan Andrews, Nikol Mitchell, Terya Trombley, Karin MacKinnon, Susan Buentello, Joy Jose, Meg Morman, Becca Knox, Caleigh Gnana-Pragasam, Alice Snyder, Marni Hamilton, Jeanine Friesen, Lysa Filcek, Anne Barbo Moon, Cheryl Wimmers, Bonnie Faville, Hellana LaRosa, Henrietta Murray, Sofia Reino, Tehara Tweed, Erin Coningsby, Sarah Rodenberg, Anita Johnson, Ligea Ruff, Stephanie Colman, Chef Annie, Alissa Hanshew, and Nicole Rogers. Quite simply, this book wouldn't exist without your diligence, patience, good humor, and support. You are the icing on my cake!

To Jenifer Ward and Emily Paster, who shared family recipes for me to adapt and include in the book. Thank you for letting me be a part of your extended families!

To my mother-in-law and father-in-law, Charlene and Mark Braun, who served as my guinea pigs from the very start of my gluten-free journey. Your love and support is something without which I would be a much lesser person.

To my sister, Laura Hollien Costanza, who is my rock and my lifelong support—I love you!

To my husband, Jeff, and my daughter, Eleanor, thank you for giving me the space and cheerleading to undertake this amazing project! I love you as high as the sky and as deep as the ocean. You are my best.

CONTENTS

FOREWORD

It's a rare cookbook that can really make a difference in people's lives. But for those who find their favorite holiday baked goods forever banished from their plates, Jeanne Sauvage's *Gluten-Free Baking for the Holidays* certainly does. Instead of simply missing out on all the cookies, desserts, and festive breads that are a treasured part of most families' celebrations, those who suffer from gluten-intolerance can now turn to Jeanne's tempting, gluten-free versions instead.

I've personally seen how the gluten Grinch can steal holiday pleasure; a close family member was diagnosed with an allergy to gluten several years ago. She could no longer enjoy any of the classic goodies our family's enthusiastic bakers routinely make and serve. No more sampling the gingerbread boys or sugar cookies or chocolate chippers that we bake with the children. No more eating the puffy dinner rolls, or tender biscuits, or turkey stuffing at Thanksgiving dinner or the pie after the meal.

In an effort to provide some substitutes, I tried to create a few gluten-free baked goods recipes myself. But even though I trained as a pastry chef and have written a number of popular baking books over the years, I haven't been thrilled with my results. With a couple of exceptions, they've been poor stand-ins for the originals I hoped to duplicate.

You see, creating recipes for tasty baked goods while eliminating gluten is wretchedly difficult—even for a professional baker. Wheat flour has long been the foundation ingredient in virtually all of our best-loved sweet treats and breads, and when it's removed, much of the traditional baking expertise must be thrown out. A new specialized body of knowledge must be painstakingly developed and employed in its place. This is where Jeanne Sauvage comes in.

Over eleven years of kitchen experimentation and study have commenced since Jeanne was diagnosed with gluten-intolerance in 2000. She has single-mindedly dedicated herself to discovering the secrets and conquering the formidable chemical challenges of baking gluten-free. Throughout, her primary goal has been to win out over the gluten Grinch by devising tempting versions of the same mainstream repertoire of treats she always baked: cookies, cakes, pies, and breads as good as they ever were, just minus that particular protein she can't eat. She's adamant about not settling for the compromised quality often found in gluten-free offerings, either for herself or for others on a similar regime. "We just lack the ability to digest gluten," she says, "not our ability to taste or enjoy good food."

I am grateful to Jeanne for her diligence and remarkable success in cracking the gluten-free baking code. This past holiday, I baked her gluten-free dinner rolls and her spiced Speculaas cookies and served them in place of my usual wheat-based versions. (Interestingly, though I know that formulating these recipes was challenging, they were remarkably straightforward and required no special baking expertise to make.) It was terrific that everybody at my table could once again enjoy the usual holiday treats together—without my having to offer any explanations or apologies, I might add. I'll be reaching for *Gluten-Free Baking for the Holidays* often in the future. If you must skip gluten or just bake for someone else who does, I think you might want to reach for it, too.

NANCY BAGGETT

INTRODUCTION
THE ROAD TO DELICIOUSNESS

I AM A LIFELONG BAKER. I WAS ONE OF THOSE TODDLERS WHO GOT UP ON A CHAIR AND WENT TO TOWN IN THE KITCHEN. I BAKED AS A KID ON WEEKENDS WHILE MY SIBLINGS PLAYED OUTSIDE; AS A HIGH SCHOOLER FOR MY PALS; IN COLLEGE AND IN GRADUATE SCHOOL AS A WAY TO AVOID STUDYING; AND AS AN ADULT TO HAVE FUN AND RELAX.

Baking has been an extremely important part of my life. Up until 2000, I baked with wheat flour. I had nary a care about the concept of gluten other than it was something you didn't want to develop too much in your pie crust or it would be tough.

Throughout this life of baking, I never paid much attention to what I called my funny tummy. I didn't feel well after most meals. I had to run to the bathroom after eating almost anything. I look back on that and wonder how I (and my doctors) could have ignored these classic signs of gluten intolerance for so long. I was put on the antidiarrhea diet, BRAT (bananas, rice, apples, toast), so many times I couldn't count them. Of course, I now know that the toast part was unhelpful in the extreme for me. During all of this, not one doctor even mentioned the concept of gluten intolerance. It was considered so rare that many doctors never bothered to learn about it because they figured they would never see a patient with it.

Little did they (or I) know that gluten intolerance is much more common than anyone ever thought. A 2003 study by the Center for Celiac Research estimated that 1 in 133 people in the United States suffers from celiac disease, the autoimmune version of gluten intolerance. When people with celiac disease ingest gluten, their body goes haywire and starts attacking itself. The small intestine is rendered unable to absorb nutrients, causing a host of medical issues such as major nutrient deficiencies, skin disorders, brain fog, and a higher incidence of certain types of cancers. This is on top of intense pain and discomfort of the digestive system. Further, in 2011, doctors at the University of Maryland School of Medicine discovered evidence of nonceliac gluten intolerance and gluten sensitivity, which seems to include most of the same symptoms. These findings indicate that the number of people who cannot tolerate gluten has nowhere to go but up.

I am one of those people. My diagnosis of nonceliac gluten intolerance finally came after the birth of my daughter in 2000. (FYI: I tested positive on the blood test for celiac disease, but I was unwilling to undergo the biopsy necessary for a true celiac diagnosis, so my technical diagnosis is nonceliac.) When I was diagnosed, I had no idea of how to cope day to day. Later, I found out that this was and is quite common for folks newly diagnosed with gluten intolerance. Most of the time, the doctors give the diagnosis, tell you that the treatment is to avoid eating gluten, and send you on your way to figure out the eating part on your own.

As you may know, gluten is a protein found in wheat, rye, and barley. Wheat is a family of grains that includes kamut, spelt, emmer, einkorn, and farro. This means that gluten is found throughout the food system. It's in many processed foods, and it's in things like soy sauce and beer. It hides via cross contamination in foods like oats, which are commonly grown and processed with gluten-containing grains. The diagnosis was something of a disaster for me at first, as it is for most newly diagnosed people. I had a new baby and was exhausted and overwhelmed, and now I couldn't eat gluten? No bread for toast and sandwiches? No pasta? No cookies or brownies? No takeout like Chinese food or pizza? What, exactly, could I eat other than rice? In the early months of new parenthood our friends brought us food to help us out, but it all contained gluten—they didn't know what to do either. I remember the lovely pie that my best friend gave us—I couldn't eat any of it, and it looked so good! Even the dinner the hospital sent home with us to congratulate us on the arrival of our new baby was lasagna—full of gluten.

Eventually, I did learn how to feed myself again and actually developed a diet that is much more full, rich, and varied than the one I had prior to my diagnosis. But I thought I would never be able to bake again. Baking was like breathing to me—I had to do it. A life without baking seemed so dreary. In the early days, I couldn't seem to find any books about gluten-free baking, and all the gluten-free baked goods I ate were not very palatable. Anything commercially available was dry and crumbly, and tasted awful. It's as if manufacturers figured that folks with gluten intolerance had lost their taste buds in addition to their ability to tolerate gluten.

After a few months of total and complete discouragement, I decided to get on with it and figure out for myself how to bake gluten-free. Since then, I have researched, experimented, and baked gluten-free, always on the search for good recipes, ingredients, and techniques. When I couldn't find good recipes, I created them. When I found wheat-based recipes I wanted to try, I adapted them to be gluten-free. Each year in this process brought more information, more knowledge, and more successful recipes. I read everything I could get my hands on about baking and about baking gluten-free. When blogs started to become more and more popular, I eagerly followed some and, ultimately, started my own (Art of Gluten-Free Baking).

I bake year-round. There isn't a week that goes by that I don't bake something. But one season that is particularly fun to bake for is the winter holiday season. I feel as if these holidays were meant for me and everyone else who loves to bake. It's a time when I can let out all the stops and bake to my heart's content. From Thanksgiving to Twelfth Night, it seems there is one festivity or another for which baking is needed. And because the holidays are times of food, family, and friends, bakers need baked goods that are so good that everyone, both those who can tolerate gluten and those who cannot, will want to eat them. There's nothing more demoralizing than bringing a baked goodie to a party or gathering, only to have everyone avoid it because it's gluten-free.

Gluten-free baking can be and is delicious baking. One of the biggest compliments I've ever gotten was from the fellow parents who came to the weekly PTA coffee hour at my daughter's school. I made a different coffee cake each week, and folks raved about each one. They asked how I made things so good. When I told people that everything was gluten-free, many of them remarked, "Wow, I guess I need to start baking gluten-free—it's much better than wheat baking."

Ultimately, baking is fun. I do it because it is one of the biggest joys in my life. As an added bonus, the results are yummy edibles. Win-win! This book concentrates on recipes for gluten-free treats whose taste and feel are indistinguishable from those of treats baked with wheat. In addition, I understand that many bakers have a need or desire to adhere to further restrictions, such as eliminating dairy, eggs, refined sugars, or grains. But, I believe that you can't begin to adapt the baking process to fit your alternative needs without first understanding how and why the basic ingredients work in the first place. Once you understand the roles that flour, eggs, fat, leaveners, and sugar play in baking, you are better able to adapt the baking process and recipes to your own needs and requirements. In this book, I discuss strategies for adapting recipes to suit you. I want to empower you to bake delicious goodies on your own terms.

I'm so happy to give you this book. I have tried to include recipes for all the treats that are traditional for celebrating the holidays between Thanksgiving and Twelfth Night. Many are based on family recipes—from my family or the families of friends.

The book is designed to be as easy to use as possible. A short gluten-free baking primer contains information about ingredients and equipment along with tables of substitutions to help you tailor the recipes to your own needs. There is a list of baking tips to help the process go more smoothly and a brief rundown on holiday baking traditions. The recipes are divided into categories of baked goods: cookies, cakes, pies and tarts, breads and crackers, and deep-fried treats. A sources section provides information on unusual ingredients and equipment. Most everything you need is available via mail order if you don't happen to have local sources.

HAPPY HOLIDAYS AND HAPPY BAKING!

01 A SHORT GLUTEN-FREE BAKING PRIMER

KNOW YOUR INGREDIENTS AND EQUIPMENT

HOLIDAY BAKING: PERMISSION TO INDULGE

BAKING IS FUN. And holiday baking is extra fun. For me, holiday baking is about complete joy. The season gives me permission to bake every day, and the constant stream of events, parties, gatherings, and meals with family and friends gives me an excuse to have baked goods covering the kitchen counters. Remember: Baking is not an extreme sport that requires perfection and lots of stress. For me, holiday baking (well, any baking really) is a stress reliever rather than a stress inducer.

Even though I bake gluten-free, I'm committed to creating excellent baked goods. Forget what you've heard about or experienced with gluten-free baking. The recipes in this book aren't good for gluten-free baked items but kind of yucky for "normal" baking. They are downright delicious and will satisfy even the most discerning palate. Just because I bake gluten-free doesn't mean I've lost my taste buds. Somehow, as gluten-free baking has developed, so has the assumption that gluten-free baked goods are fairly icky. Oddly, people often think that I am willing to eat just about anything as long as it's gluten-free. Well, forget it. I will only eat something if it tastes good and feels right. Therefore, with my recipes, if something isn't amazing, it's back to the drawing board. In the words of my friend Kim, "There's no point in eating something that's not yummy." So bake away and know that no matter who eats what you make or where (at the family dinner table or at the school play reception), everyone will happily clear the plate and probably ask you for the recipe.

INGREDIENTS

I start where any baker worth her salt starts; with excellent ingredients. Excellent baked goods can't be made out of poor-quality ingredients. This isn't meant to be preachy—it's just a fact. For me, this means using organic whenever possible and using as few artificial ingredients as possible. Look for organic flours, as well as organic butter and eggs, and for pure extracts like vanilla, almond, peppermint, anise, and lemon. Folks often have multiple food allergies and intolerances (I know I do). So, if you need to use substitutions, choose the best ones you can find, such as organic butter substitutes or good-quality flax seeds. Making your own baked goods is much cheaper than buying premade ones, so invest the savings in high-quality ingredients.

This brief rundown on the basic building blocks of baking will help you know what ingredients do what, whether you are a brand-new baker or an experienced baker new to gluten-free baking. In addition, this information will enable you to make informed decisions about how to substitute ingredients if and when needed.

First and foremost: The primary difference between wheat baking and gluten-free baking is that gluten-free flours don't have gluten. This is an obvious statement, but it's the best place to start. Almost everything else about the two types of baking is pretty much the same. The same other ingredients, the same basic techniques, the same equipment. I point this out because many people assume that gluten-free baking is a whole other animal from wheat baking, and that causes them to panic.

The top five ingredients in baking (including gluten-free baking) are flour, eggs, fats and oils, leaveners, and sugar. Once you know the role that each plays in baking, you will understand the importance of each in gluten-free baking.

FLOURS

In baking, flour provides one of the most important elements: structure. Without it, baked goods would have no shape or crumb. Thus, using the right flour is important. For wheat baking, choosing flour is easy—you just have to select the grade of flour you want to use, for example, pastry, bread, cake, or all-purpose. But for gluten-free baking, flours are more complicated. For one thing, there is a whole host of flours to choose from, and each has different properties to be aware of. Wheat flour is a mix of protein, starch, and gums. For gluten-free baking, we need to find gluten-free replacements that mimic the properties of each of those elements. Most bakers have come to agree that no single gluten-free flour works well by itself. Some are high in starch. Some are high in protein. None really have the gums that we need. And none have the magic binder and structure builder, gluten. Please note that it is important to buy flours labeled "gluten free." Sometimes a naturally gluten-free flour is processed using the same equipment as gluten-containing products, and as a result is not gluten-free.

Gluten is made up of two proteins: glutenin and gliadin. Glutenin is shaped like a squiggle, and gliadin is shaped like a spiral. When water is added to wheat flour and the resulting dough is manipulated, these two proteins become more and more interlocked. By this process, gluten in the flour creates a skeleton structure for baked items. Then the starches in the flour come into play and adhere to this structure like a skin, creating something of a tent covering. It's this covering that the gases from the leaveners push against to raise the structure of the baked products to their intended height and shape without falling. Without gluten, there is no structural skeleton for the starches to adhere to, and the resulting baked goods are flat and crumbly, and don't hold their shape.

What's more, gluten is a very specific kind of protein that is strong yet elastic—which means it can be stretched and will return to its original shape. Or it can be coaxed into holding different shapes. And, it can be manipulated, so that adding more water to the dough and doing more mixing or kneading will create a stronger structure. Gluten is quite an amazing substance, and mimicking its properties has been the number-one challenge for gluten-free baking.

One of the biggest problems for gluten-free baking is that no single gluten-free flour mimics wheat flour. Thus, we've had to accept and work under a different paradigm than that of wheat baking. Whereas with wheat baking you just pull out one bag of flour when you want to bake, with gluten-free baking you need to pull out more than one flour.

I have found that the concept of using more than one flour contributes to the general sense that gluten-free baking is more complicated than wheat baking. It's really not. It just requires more flour bags in the pantry. Some bakers like to tweak their baking flours for each recipe. I don't. My goal has always been to mimic, as much as possible, wheat flour. Wheat flour comes in different grades for different projects. But for 80 percent of what is baked in the home kitchen, all-purpose wheat flour is used. So, after much trial and effort, I have come up with one basic gluten-free all-purpose flour mix that does quite well for most of my general baking. To me, mixing up flours so they can be kept on hand as you would a bag of wheat flour is preferable to measuring out several different flours for each baking session.

The mix that I have developed, with the scintillating name Jeanne's Gluten-Free All-Purpose Flour, closely mimics the properties of unbleached all-purpose wheat flour. I have researched the composition of all-purpose wheat flour (because I am a baking nerd) and have found that about 80 percent of wheat flour is composed of starches and about 20 percent is composed of proteins. Of importance is that the protein in all-purpose wheat flour is not just any protein—it's mostly a specific kind of protein, gluten. So, a gluten-free mix that is mostly starch with some protein is the best type of mix to use in order to mimic the wheat texture.

In addition, my mix includes xanthan gum, which is considered to be a gluten replacer. I have found that no matter how much I mess around with the protein content of the flours alone, I can't quite get the gluten effect. Something has to be added as the final, gluten-simulating element. In my experience, xanthan gum does the best job at this. There are many different types of gluten replacers on the market—guar gum, flax seeds, chia seeds, and psyllium seeds—and different bakers prefer different ones. What they all have in common is that they are forms of water-soluble fiber, which means that they can absorb many times their weight in water. This helps them act like the gums in wheat flour. In addition, they all have, to some degree, binding and structure-building properties. Where

xanthan gum excels is in elasticity. Xanthan gum does a pretty good job, and a much better job than the other gluten replacers, at allowing the shape of the baked good to be manipulated and held. Guar gum does a bit of this, although it is much less elastic. The seeds provide binding properties, but not the structure or elastic properties. Therefore, the seeds do a better job of replacing eggs in a baked product than replacing gluten.

All the gluten replacers are dietary fiber. This means that any of them, eaten in large quantities, may create gastric disturbances if you're not used to it. One thing I like about xanthan gum is that a little goes a long way. For most regular baking, you only need a scant ¼ tsp per 1 cup/140 g gluten-free flour. By comparison, you need to use more guar gum or seeds. Also, contrary to a lot of misinformation, xanthan gum is a natural product. It is derived from a bacteria that is grown on a sugar medium (which makes it kind of like yeast).

JEANNE'S GLUTEN-FREE ALL-PURPOSE FLOUR
MAKES 4½ CUPS / 660 G

1¼ cups/170 g brown rice flour
1¼ cups/205 g white rice flour
1 cup/165 g sweet rice flour
1 cup/120 g tapioca flour
scant 2 tsp xanthan gum

In a large bowl, whisk together the brown and white rice flours, sweet rice flour, tapioca flour, and xanthan gum thoroughly. Transfer the mix to an airtight container. Store in a cool, dark place for up to 6 weeks or in the refrigerator for up to 4 months.

My gluten-free all-purpose mix is a combination of brown rice flour, white rice flour, sweet (or glutinous) rice flour, and tapioca flour. This mix achieves several objectives: it mimics the protein to starch ratio in wheat flour; it uses mild-tasting flours that do not interfere with the taste of the resulting baked product; it contains no common allergens (specifically nuts, corn, or potato); and it calls for flours that are relatively easy to find (see Sources for Ingredients & Equipment).

If you want to substitute flours in this mix, do so by flour category. See the following table for specific flour substitution ideas.

COMPONENTS OF MY MIX	PROPERTIES	SUGGESTED SUBSTITUTE
Brown rice flour	Whole grain, a bit gritty, adds some flavor	Sorghum flour
White rice flour	Bleached flour, adds neutral structure and smoothness	Millet flour
Tapioca flour (also known as tapioca starch)	Starchy, adds smoothness and binding capabilities	Potato starch (not potato flour)
Sweet rice flour (also known as glutinous rice flour)	Starchy, adds smoothness and thickening capabilities	Potato flour (not potato starch)
Xanthan gum	Gluten replacer	Guar gum

I have noticed that some people are more sensitive than others to the grind of certain flours, particularly brown rice flour. If this is you, I recommend using a brown rice flour labeled "superfine." Also, some people feel that

different types of tapioca flour (starch) taste different from each other. If this is you, do some experimenting to see what brand tastes best. Be sure that any flour you use is labeled "gluten free." Sometimes naturally gluten-free flours are cross-contaminated with gluten flours.

Several commercially available gluten-free flour mixes on the market are similar to mine if you do not want to make your own mix. When choosing one, look for a mix that has xanthan gum already included. Or be sure to add ¼ tsp xanthan gum per 1 cup/140 g flour. Also, if you choose a mix that contains bean flour, be aware that your final baked product will taste like bean.

EGGS

The next most important structure-building ingredient in baking is eggs. Because gluten-free baked goods require help in the structure department, I always use extra-large eggs because they provide an extra boost. In addition to being structure builders, eggs are binders—they help keep the resulting baked goods together.

If you are intolerant of or sensitive to chicken eggs, I recommend (after speaking with your doctor) that you try duck eggs in your baking. Duck eggs are larger than

EGG AND EGG REPLACERS	
1 extra-large egg	¼ cup/ 60 ml liquid (an extra-large egg is equal to ¼ cup/60ml of liquid)
1 extra-large egg	1 duck egg
1 extra-large egg	1 Tbsp ground flax seed plus 3 Tbsp hot water, whisked together and allowed to sit for 15 minutes

chicken eggs and provide even more structure and binding properties. Substitute one duck egg for each extra-large chicken egg. If you can't tolerate any eggs, you have to experiment with other ingredients that will somewhat mimic the action of eggs. Please note that there isn't any ideal egg substitute, so your baked goods will behave a bit differently if you use one.

BUTTER AND DAIRY PRODUCTS

The most popular fat in baking is butter. This is because it does the best job at giving baked goods their smooth mouthfeel and appealing taste. In this book and in all my baking, I call for unsalted butter. I like to be able to control

BUTTER AND DAIRY REPLACERS

Butter	Nondairy butter replacer or margarine. If the replacer is extra salty, delete the salt in the recipe.
Milk	Nondairy milk (rice, almond, hemp, soy). Make sure it is labeled "gluten free."
Buttermilk	1 cup/240 ml nondairy milk mixed with 1 Tbsp vinegar = 1 cup buttermilk
Cream	⅔ cup/165 ml nondairy milk mixed with ⅓ cup/75 ml melted butter substitute = 1 cup/240 ml cream. **NOTE:** *This mixture will not whip like dairy cream.*
Evaporated milk	4 cups/1 L nondairy milk simmered on low for 2 hours = 2½ cups / 600 ml evaporated milk (Watch carefully so mixture doesn't burn.)

the amount of salt in my baked goods, so I add salt as a separate ingredient. If you can't use butter, I recommend an organic nonhydrogenated butter substitute or margarine. Please note that many butter replacers are quite salty. If this is the case with the one you use, delete the salt from recipes. Also, most butter substitutes are softer than butter at room temperature. Several recipes in this book, such as the Cutout Cookies (page 56), rely on the butter to retain the shape of the items during the initial part of baking. Therefore, when using a butter substitute, refrigerate the cookies so that they firm up before baking.

Many recipes in this book contain milk or cream as the liquid component. Dairy milk is the best, again because of its superb mouthfeel. But if you can't use dairy, see the table at left for substitutes.

OIL

Several recipes in this book call for deep-frying or require a neutral-tasting oil. I use rice bran oil. It has a high smoke point, which makes it terrific for deep-frying. It has a bland taste, which doesn't interfere with the other flavors in a recipe, and it is hypoallergenic. If you don't want to use rice bran oil, canola oil is a good substitute. Keep in mind that deep-fried foods don't retain nearly the amount of oil that people think they do, so don't let the fear of excess oil get in the way of making the deep-fried treats in this book.

I always get questions on how to dispose of oil after deep-frying. Please be aware that most deep-frying oil may be used more than once. Most of the time, I use mine twice. When the oil is completely cool, I pour the oil through a fine-mesh colander to strain out the food particles and then transfer the oil to a glass jar and store in the refrigerator. I try to use it within two weeks. I then dispose of the oil in an environmentally (and house) safe way. First, cool the oil completely for safety's sake (never dispose of hot or warm oil). Next, pour it into an old milk carton or plastic container, seal well, and place in the garbage can. I don't use glass because it may break in the garbage. Never pour large quantities of oil down the drain—it will clog the pipes and create problems for the environment. If you use large quantities of oil, a local restaurant may be willing to let you pour the oil into its waste receptacle for oil.

LEAVENERS

Yeast, baking soda, and baking powder, the leaveners used in baking, create the lovely air holes and pockets that give baked items their texture. Leaveners help produce gases or steam that works on the air pockets to push up against the structure created by the flour, gums, eggs, and sugar in doughs. Different leaveners are used in different types of baked items, but all create light, fluffy results. Some recipes, like cookies and flat crackers, use little or no leaveners; others, like cakes and bread, use more.

Baking powder is one of the most important leaveners for everyday gluten-free baking because it works during the mixing process, when it comes into contact with the liquid in batters and doughs, and again in the baking process, when heat is applied. For this reason, most commercial baking powders are called double acting. Gluten-free batters and doughs are a bit less pliable than wheat batters and doughs, and extra leavener is needed to create good air pockets. Thus, many gluten-free recipes for breads,

muffins, and biscuits will call for more baking powder than do wheat recipes. Homemade baking powder is single acting and won't be as powerful as commercial double-acting powder.

In the past, some baking powders were cut with wheat starch. Today, most of the popular and readily available baking powders use cornstarch or potato starch. Just to be sure, read the labels of any baking powder you choose. Also, please note the expiration date on your baking powder. An expired baking powder is not dangerous, but it will be weaker.

Baking soda is often used in tandem with baking powder. The leavening action of baking soda is triggered by acidic ingredients, commonly vinegar, buttermilk, honey, and brown sugar. You will often find baking soda by itself in cookies, which need just a bit of rising power. Baking soda by itself is often not strong enough to help gluten-free cakes, muffins, or breads rise.

The special property of yeast is that it is a collection of living organisms, or fungi, and its rising capabilities are prodigious and malleable. You can manipulate yeast and make it rise your baked goods in many different ways and amounts. The yeast I use in this book is active dry yeast (not fast acting or cake). It is available in large bags, jars, and little packets. For the casual home baker, I recommend the jarred yeast available at grocery stores for its ease of measuring. The amount of yeast used in gluten-free recipes is several times more than the amount used in wheat baking. Therefore, the little packets, each measuring about 2¼ tsp, are inconvenient. If you are an avid bread baker, you may want to order yeast in large bags. Most baking yeasts are gluten-free, but check the label on the yeast you use to make sure.

SUGAR

In addition to making baked items sweet, sugar serves various essential functions. It acts as a leavener by helping to incorporate air bubbles into the batter during the beating step. In addition, sugar acts as a preservative, allowing baked goods to last longer than they normally would without sugar. This is why many commercial baked items are overly sweet. Sugar attracts water, creating a fine crumb in cakes, muffins, and quick breads. This property also causes the tops of muffins and cakes to become gummy when stored for long periods. (The high percentage of sugar is what helps cookies become crisp.)

For my baking, I use three kinds of sugar: granulated, confectioners' (powdered), and brown, specifically dark brown. I prefer organic sugars for their more complex taste. I think dark brown sugar tastes better than light brown, but you may use either depending upon your preference.

The most commonly available sugar is cane sugar, made from sugar cane. If you can't use cane sugar, there are alternatives. Beet granulated sugar is interchangeable with cane granulated sugar. Palm sugar, another nice alternative, comes in different forms, such as granulated and cake. It has a deeper, more prevalent flavor than cane granulated sugar. Maple sugar is yet another option, although the resulting baked items will have a faint maple taste (which isn't necessarily a bad thing). Experiment with these sugars to find out what you like best.

SALT AND SPICES

Used often in baking, salt suppresses bitterness and provides a foil to sweetness. A sweet baked item is not nearly as good without salt. I prefer fine sea salt for most of my baking because of the way it tastes. Sea salt contains trace minerals that give it a more complex flavor. In addition, I sometimes use kosher salt, a type of coarse salt, for certain recipes when I want to amplify the salt flavor.

Winter holiday baking tends to include many spices. Where possible, I like to grind my own. I do this most often with nutmeg—freshly ground nutmeg is far better than preground nutmeg. You can also grind your own allspice and coriander. I grind most of my spices with a coffee grinder. I rarely drink coffee, so I use the same grinder that I use for grinding coffee beans, but I clean it carefully between uses. If your grinder gets regular use for coffee, you may want to invest in a second grinder for spices. For nutmeg, you can also use a nutmeg grinder or a Microplane grater (see page 25).

EQUIPMENT FOR THE GLUTEN-FREE HOLIDAY BAKING KITCHEN

Baking is one of those enterprises where you can go absolutely crazy buying equipment, or you can get by quite nicely with a few key tools. I, of course, am on the side of being crazy over equipment. Only the size of my small kitchen and my pocketbook hold me back. Winter holiday baking is its own world, and some of the recipes (but by no means all) require specialized equipment. Thus, for holiday baking you can go even more crazy acquiring equipment. The following list includes items from the most common and often used to the extremely specialized. Don't be overwhelmed—the list is thorough so that you can see why I recommend each item and then decide what you feel you need.

OVEN THERMOMETER

If you don't have one, get one immediately! Seriously, I can't tell you how many of my readers report a baking failure that ultimately turns out to be inaccurate oven temperature. Most ovens, no matter how fancy or new, don't heat to the temperature that they say they do. Some run high; some run low; some are erratic. Regardless, baking something at the wrong temperature has the potential to turn a fun baking session into a disappointing failure. Oven thermometers are relatively cheap and widely accessible (I got mine at the local drugstore). I recommend that you get one and put it in your oven. It can live there full-time (mine does).

CANDY THERMOMETER

This is a must-have for deep-frying. Deep-fried items in this book are delicious and include jelly doughnuts, pumpkin doughnuts, rosettes, cannoli, *struffoli*, and *buñuelos*. I use a thermometer with a dial face because I find it easier to read than the vertical mercury versions.

INSTANT-READ THERMOMETER

I have come to feel that this inexpensive gadget is invaluable when baking yeast breads. Yeast is best proofed (allowed to grow to prove its viability) in water that is about 110°F/43°C. Also, I have never been able to hear whether or not a yeast bread sounds "hollow" when done, the typical cue that you read in cookbooks. But now I don't have to—as long as the bread reaches an internal temperature of about 190°F/88°C, I know it's baked through!

MEASURING CUPS AND SPOONS

For dry ingredients, I like to use good-quality metal measuring cups and spoons. They are durable and last longer than plastic. I have two sets of each. For liquids, I have several glass cup measures in various sizes, the most helpful being the 2-cup/480-ml measure. This cup is big enough for most home baking projects without being too big.

There's been a fair amount of talk about using a scale to weigh ingredients versus measuring ingredients by volume. Measuring by volume (such as cups) has been standard in the United States and works fine. The margin of error in measuring is fairly large for home bakers. So being off by a small amount here and there when measuring by volume isn't the end of the world. One thing that is important when measuring by volume is to use top-notch metal cups and spoons.

SCALE

The practice of measuring ingredients by weight rather than volume is more common outside the United States. This book gives measurements by weight in addition to volume. If you prefer to weigh ingredients, get a scale that measures in ounces and grams, and has a tare (or zero) function. The scale should allow you to weigh ingredients in single-gram increments. Until recently, home scales often measured in 5-gram increments.

HEAVY-DUTY STAND MIXER

My heavy-duty stand mixer is the one thing I use almost every time I bake. I wouldn't do without it. The fats, oils, and eggs in gluten-free batters and doughs need to be beaten well in order to have sufficient air bubbles in which the leaveners do their rising. I highly recommend that you take the plunge and get a good-quality heavy-duty stand mixer. If your budget is limited, look for a refurbished product on company Web sites (that's where I found mine) and for sales. Sites like eBay always have used equipment at good prices. I recommend that you get a mixer that has at least a 5-qt/4.7-L capacity and comes with whisk, paddle, and dough hook attachments.

ELECTRIC HAND MIXER

Even though I am a huge fan of my stand mixer, I once used a hand mixer for all my heavy mixing, and it worked just fine. If you are a casual baker, or you can't yet afford a stand mixer, a good-quality hand mixer is an excellent alternative. If you want the best of both worlds, get a hand mixer in addition to your stand mixer. I use the hand mixer for small baking projects. It's also handy as an extra mixer when I have two things going for one recipe; for example, beating the butter for the dough with the stand mixer and beating the cream for the topping with the hand mixer.

FOOD PROCESSOR OR BLENDER

These are helpful tools in the gluten-free baking kitchen. If you can swing it, I recommend one or the other; but, you can get away without either. I do have a food processor, and I love it. It helps cut together ingredients quickly for flaky pastries, and it chops nuts in seconds. However, I don't use it enough to recommend it as a must-have.

BAKING PANS

As you can imagine, I have lots of pans. Way more than any one person really needs. Most successful baking is done in light-colored metal or glass pans. Light-colored metal is best because it reflects the heat instead of absorbing it, as dark-colored metal pans do. And, with the exception of pie pans, I don't recommend using pans made out of pottery. If you bake with glass pans, you will probably find that your baking time needs to be increased by 5 to 10 minutes. This is because glass takes longer to heat up and to conduct heat.

I will admit that I am not a fan of nonstick pans. I have found that the majority of nonstick pans are not really nonstick, and that the nonstick coating on the cheap pans tends to degrade over time and flake off. I have to replace nonstick pans on a regular basis, while pans that are not nonstick are still performing well. That said, some pans seem only available in nonstick form, including six-cup muffin pans and metal Bundt pans.

Following are the pans in this book and the recipes that use them.

Square and Rectangular Baking Pans / An 8-in/20-cm square pan is one of the most handy pans to have in the kitchen. It is used for the Toasted Pecan Snack Cake (page 93), Gingerbread Cake with Persimmon (page 82), and Lemon Bars (page 66). Cinnamon Rolls (page 118) are baked in a rectangular pan measuring 9 by 13 in/ 23 by 33 cm.

Round Pan / I use an 8- or 9-in/20- or 23-cm round pan for the Featherlight Buttermilk Biscuits (page 122).

Half Sheet Pan / Measuring 18 by 12 in/46 by 30.5 cm, this extremely handy pan doubles as a cookie sheet. I have two half sheet pans in my kitchen. In addition to baking with them, I often use them as staging or rising areas for different recipes. You will need one to make the Genoise for the Bûche de Noël (page 75).

Loaf Pan / A standard loaf pan is 9 by 5 in/23 by 12 cm. I have two in my kitchen because I bake a lot of bread. You will need a loaf pan for the Soft Sandwich Bread (page 125) and Date Nut Bread (page 126).

Pie Pans / I prefer glass or pottery pie pans. Glass is the best. It conducts heat slowly and steadily and is well suited to pie making. Pottery pie pans conduct heat well, too, and are pretty. I used a 9-in/23-cm glass Pyrex pan and a pottery Emile Henry pan of the same size to test the pie recipes in this book except for the Chocolate-Sunflower Butter Pie (page 104) and the Shortbread Cookies (page 52), for which I used a 10-in/25-cm pan. A metal pan, especially a dark metal one, is the worst performer when it comes to pies.

Bundt Pan / I love to make coffee cakes, and Bundt pans are fun to bake with. They come in a variety of shapes and sizes. The Orange-Scented Olive Oil Cake (page 85) and Chocolate-Mandarin Cake (page 83) are designed to be baked in Bundt pans with a capacity of at least 9 to 10 cups/2.1 to 2.4 L.

Muffin Pans / Many recipes in this book, including those for muffins, have nonstandard yields. I recommend getting one standard muffin pan with 12 cups and one standard muffin pan with 6 cups. These will be used for the Dinner Rolls (page 121), Applesauce Spice Muffins (page 117), and Fortune Cookies (page 45). The Mincemeat Tarts (page 107) are baked in a 24-cup mini-muffin pan.

Springform Pan / This pan with removable sides is handy when you're making something that is unwieldy to turn out of another baking pan. The standard springform is 9½ or 10 in/24 or 25 cm in diameter. You will use this pan for the Fruitcake (page 78) and Cranberry Cake (page 81).

Tube Pan / This pan is also known as an angel food cake pan. Some versions have a removable bottom; others don't. Either is fine. A 9-in/23-cm tube pan is used for the King Cake (page 86) and Pound Cake (page 89).

Cookie Sheets / I highly recommend getting large, heavy, good-quality cookie sheets, typically about 17 by 14 in/43 by 35.5 cm or 18 by 12 in/46 by 30.5 cm. They should be made of light-colored metal and, ideally, should not be nonstick if you can swing it. Two sheets are nice to have. This way you can bake one batch of cookies while preparing another batch. You can also use half-sheet pans as cookie sheets.

Cast-Iron Skillet / I love my cast-iron skillet. I use it for many things, including baking. Once it is seasoned, a cast-iron pan is almost nonstick. And treated well, it will last forever. A 10-in/25-cm pan is used for the Skillet Cornbread (page 124).

WIRE COOLING RACKS

A large-grid cooling rack measuring 10 by 18 in/25 by 46 cm is a must for baking. I recommend having two racks.

They are useful not only for cooling baked goods, but also for holding frosted cookies while the glaze drips off. If you are an avid cookie baker, you might want to spring for a set of stacked cooling racks that allow you to cool many batches of cookies at once in a small space. I have a small kitchen, and I have a set of these. They are lifesavers at holiday time!

PASTRY BRUSH

Amazingly, this is one of my most-used baking tools. I have three, and I rotate through them almost every day. Because gluten-free dough is so sticky, I often recommend that you grease and flour pans because greasing alone isn't effective enough. My method is to melt a bit of butter in the microwave and then brush it on the pan with a pastry brush. Next I spoon in a bit of tapioca flour and shake the pan around in order to completely cover the interior surface before shaking out the excess flour. I have two types of brushes: silicone and boar's hair. The silicone brush is much more durable, while the hair brush is useful on delicate baked goods.

ROLLING PIN

Every baker needs a rolling pin. And the number of rolling pins on the market is astounding. Of them, my favorite is the French tapered wood rolling pin. When I roll out dough with a standard pin, I press hard on the ends, where my hands are stationed, which tends to leave a hump of thicker dough in the middle. The tapered pin reduces the unevenness, leading to more uniformly rolled dough. But, I am not one to reject your family rolling pin. If you have one that you like and works well for you, by all means stick with it.

MICROPLANE GRATER/ZESTER

This tool gets a workout in my kitchen. I use it for zesting citrus, shredding cheese, and grating whole nutmeg. It is also good for evening the edges of the Gingerbread House (page 67). For some weird reason, I get a thrill every time I use mine. I'm a baking nerd to the Nth degree.

COOKIE CUTTERS

Holiday baking wouldn't be complete without cookie cutters. I have dozens of cutters, including stars, trees, bells, angels, people, dreidels, and snowflakes. I also recommend cookie cutter sets. I have a set of round cutters in various sizes, which are useful for biscuits as well as cookies, and a set of star cutters in various sizes. These two sets can get you a very long way.

DOUGHNUT CUTTER

If you make doughnuts on a regular basis, a doughnut cutter is a handy tool. The one I have is 2½ in/6.5 cm in diameter on the outside, with an attached inner cutter that is 1 in/2.5 cm in diameter. A doughnut cutter is used for the Pumpkin Doughnuts (page 138).

PASTRY CUTTER OR PIZZA WHEEL

This item comes in handy when you need to cut out large quantities of dough shapes. I use the cutter when I cut out the molded shapes for Springerle (page 38) and the dough wedges for Rugelach (page 42).

TAPE MEASURE OR RULER

So much of baking involves rolling dough out to certain measurements. I use a regular tape measure from the hardware store for this. A ruler works well, too.

PASTRY BAG AND TIPS

A few recipes require piping icing or meringue into shapes or patterns, particularly for the Gingerbread House (page 67), Gingerbread Cookies (page 59), and Meringue Mushrooms (page 62). The beauty of a pastry bag is that you can use the various tips that come in a simple kit to achieve different looks for decorating. The kits are inexpensive, but you can often get away with making a pastry bag by snipping off the corner of a lock-top plastic bag. I do this all the time, and it works just fine.

PARCHMENT PAPER

Over the years, I've switched from greasing my cookie sheets to lining them with parchment paper. I bake so often that using parchment paper significantly cuts down on cleanup. Although a Silpat Nonstick Baking Mat can be used instead of parchment paper, it adds 3 to 5 minutes to your baking time. I compost as many things as I can, and certain kinds of unbleached parchment paper are compostable.

WAXED PAPER

Where possible, I use two pieces of waxed paper for rolling out my cookie and pie doughs. Gluten-free dough is sticky. It's more sticky than wheat flour dough because the xanthan gum is activated right away with the addition of liquid to the dough, and xanthan gum is sticky. Many recipes in this book are rolled out, so I often recommend waxed paper. It's less messy than flouring a work surface and therefore reduces cleanup time. A few recipes, the Stollen (page 130) in particular, are so sticky that a heavily floured surface is more useful for rolling than waxed paper.

SILPAT NONSTICK BAKING MAT

I don't use my Silpat Nonstick Baking Mat that much. The one recipe I do recommend using it for in this book is the Fortune Cookies (page 45). The dough is so sticky that the Silpat mat is the best baking surface, although a very well-greased surface will work, too.

SPECIALTY EQUIPMENT

Some holiday recipes require unusual baking equipment not normally stocked in most kitchens. I find these irons, molds, and presses fun to use, because when I need to pull out one of the items, I know that the holidays are here and it's time to get busy baking.

Krumkake Iron and Pizzelle Iron / *Krumkake* are Scandinavian thin waffle cookies, and *pizzelles* are Italian thin waffle cookies. Each type of iron imprints a traditional design onto the waffles. The irons often come with cone rollers (for *krumkake*) or cylinder rollers (for *pizzelles*), which allow you to roll the waffles into cones or tubes that can be filled with whipped cream or another fluffy confection. *Krumkake* are more traditionally rolled than are *pizzelles*. Traditionally, *krumkake* are a bit thinner than *pizzelles*, and each type of waffle cookie has a different design, so technically the irons are not interchangeable. If you want to be authentic, you need to have both irons.

Rosette Iron / A Scandinavian holiday delicacy, rosettes are extremely thin, delicate deep-fried pastries. They are often compared to American funnel cakes. They are made from shaped irons that resemble branding irons. The irons are dipped in batter and immediately placed in hot oil. Older rosette irons are made of cast iron. If you can get your hands on a set (say, at a garage sale or on eBay), do it. If not, the modern cast-aluminum sets are fine.

Springerle and Speculaas Cookie Molds / *Springerle* are German anise-scented cakey cookies, and *speculaas* are Dutch spice cookies. They are made by imprinting their respective doughs with specially cut molds. The molds range in size and complexity, and each is more beautiful than the next. Traditionally, *springerle* molds are smooth inside the designs, while *speculaas* molds have a distinctive ridged pattern inside the designs. There are also rolling pins with the molds etched into them, so you can roll the shapes onto the dough. To make authentic *springerle* cookies, you need a *springerle* mold. You may use regular cookie cutters for the *speculaas*.

Panettone Molds / A traditional Italian yeasted sweet bread, panettone is frequently made at holiday times. The most common shape is a large cylinder. Panettone is most often baked in special disposable paper molds. The most common size is 6 by 4 in/15 by 10 cm.

Steamed Pudding Mold / This mold for holding pudding batter, with a capacity of about 2 qt/2 L, is designed to be set on a steamer in a stockpot partially filled with water.

You want a pudding mold that has a lid. In years past, some cookbooks recommended using clean coffee cans covered with aluminum foil as molds. I strongly advise against this practice. Most cans (at least in the United States) have the potential of being lined with a toxic plastic, bisphenol A (BPA), that is activated by heat. If you want to use a can, check its BPA status first.

Cookie Press / This handy, time-saving tool is filled with a butter-based dough, fitted with a shaping disk, and then used to press out dough shapes onto a cookie sheet. My cookie press has twenty shaping disks, meaning that it can create twenty different cookie shapes.

Cannoli Tubes / The reusable metal tubes are 5½ by ⅞ in/ 14 by 2 cm and usually come four to a pack. They are designed to be wrapped with cannoli dough and then submerged in hot oil to allow the cannoli to cook into a tube shape. After the cannoli are cooked, the tubes are removed and used again.

Trifle Bowl / This big glass bowl, often with a pedestal, is for making trifle and other layered desserts, where you want to show off the different elements. My bowl is standard, about 8½ in/21.5 cm in diameter and 5 in/12 cm deep.

STORING GLUTEN-FREE BAKED GOODS

This is definitely an area where you will notice the differences between wheat and gluten-free baked items. One of the most important rules of thumb: Most gluten-free items don't do well in the refrigerator after baking—they dry out too easily. But sugar is a preservative, so baked treats last a bit longer at room temperature than you might think. I recommend that you monitor your own experiences and get a sense for how your own baked goods store in your kitchen.

One way to combat the problem of gluten-free baked goods drying out quickly or becoming gummy is to microwave them for a few seconds before serving. Breads are nice toasted the day after baking.

Some doughs can be made in advance and stored until used. Keep nonyeasted cookie dough in an airtight container in the refrigerator for several days or freeze for up to 6 months. Yeasted dough can be refrigerated for up to 24 hours before baking. Cake batter should be used the day it is mixed, but can be refrigerated in the bowl, tightly covered, for a few hours before baking. The batter for doughnuts can be kept in the refrigerator for 48 hours.

All the recipes in this book provide instructions for short-term storage. Some baked goods can be frozen successfully. Cookies can be wrapped well in plastic wrap and frozen for up to 6 months; defrost them overnight in the refrigerator. Yeasted breads, wrapped tightly in plastic wrap, can be frozen for up to 6 weeks; defrost all frozen items overnight in the refrigerator.

These are things I've learned over the years that help gluten-free baking be as successful as it can be. Most of the tips are true for successful baking in general.

1 / READ THE RECIPE BEFORE STARTING

It takes only a couple of minutes and is so helpful. This way, there are no middle-of-the-recipe surprises.

2 / GATHER YOUR INGREDIENTS AND TOOLS

This is called *mise-en-place* (everything in place) and also includes reading your recipe in advance. Assembling what you need ahead is easier than running around the kitchen trying to find everything as you go along. Review the recipe, gather all the ingredients and tools, and set them out where you will use them. Ah, so much more relaxing.

3 / HEAT YOUR OVEN TO THE CORRECT TEMPERATURE

This is easy to do—get an oven thermometer and keep it in your oven. Then check it every time you bake to make sure the oven temperature is what it needs to be.

4 / PREHEAT YOUR OVEN WELL

Over the years, I've learned to preheat my oven a bit longer than most people do theirs, because I want to make sure my oven is evenly hot. As the oven preheats, I watch my oven thermometer to confirm that the oven interior is at the temperature I need it to be.

5 / BRING YOUR INGREDIENTS TO ROOM TEMPERATURE

I always bring ingredients, particularly butter and eggs, to room temperature unless the recipe specifies otherwise. This ensures that the batter or dough mixes together well. If you decide to make something at the last minute, you can soften butter by putting it in the microwave for a few seconds, and you can place eggs, still in their shells, in warm (not hot) water for about 10 minutes.

6 / FLUFF YOUR FLOUR BEFORE YOU MEASURE

This is fairly easy with a gluten-free flour mix. Since you have to mix it anyway, it will probably be fluffed up with no extra effort on your part. If you haven't used the mix for a while, give it a few stirs with a whisk before measuring.

7 / KNOW HOW TO MEASURE

If you measure ingredients by volume, be as accurate as you can. Dip your measuring cup into the flour, bring it level over the flour container, and lightly tap the cup on the side of the container (this applies to gluten-free flours, which are light and prone to static electricity). Then sweep off the excess flour above the top of the cup rim with a straight edge (I use the back of a knife). If you measure ingredients by weight, know how to work your scale and be sure you're not measuring the weight of your container along with the weight of your ingredients.

8 / BEAT AIR INTO YOUR FATS

This is very important for light and fluffy gluten-free cakes, muffins, and pies. Leaveners such as baking soda and baking powder don't create their own air pockets in baked goods but work on the air pockets already formed by the mixing process. Fat, usually butter, and then the fat and sugar need to be beaten well to create as many air pockets as possible. This is why almost every recipe in this book gives the timing for beating butter. Gluten-free baked goods tend to be a bit heavy and dense, and the extra time spent creating air pockets eliminates this problem. Don't skip it!

9 / BEAT EGG WHITES WITHOUT ANY FAT

Be very careful when you separate eggs whites from yolks when making meringue. Just a tiny bit of yolk will add enough fat to make the whites not beat as high as needed. Also make sure that your bowl and beaters are clean and free of fats such as butter. There is nothing more depressing than meringue that doesn't form.

10 / FLOUR YOUR PANS AND ROLLING BOARD WITH TAPIOCA FLOUR

Do not use gluten-free flour mix, because the xanthan gum in the mix is activated by liquid. Therefore, the flour mix will make the dough adhere to the pans or board. I flour my pans and rolling surface with tapioca flour. The flour is fine so it won't add a gritty feel to the exterior of your baked goods as other flours might.

11 / GREASE *AND* FLOUR YOUR PANS

When not lining pans with unbleached parchment paper, I grease and flour pans instead of just greasing them (see page 25). The xanthan gum in gluten-free flour mix tends to make the batters adhere to the surfaces of pans, especially Bundt pans, which have lots of nooks and crannies.

12 / USE THE MIDDLE OVEN RACK

Every recipe in this book was tested with the rack positioned in the middle of the oven, the optimal place for baking. The exception is when I'm baking Meringue Mushrooms (page 62) and when I'm crunched for time and need to bake more than one sheet of cookies at a time. Then I will place the sheets on the middle and bottom racks. Otherwise, do not place your baking pans anywhere but the middle rack. That's just asking for uneven baking.

13 / DON'T BE AFRAID OF DEEP-FRYING

Deep-frying is quite straightforward, and the recipes in this book that call for deep-frying all have detailed directions on how to do it. One trick no one seems to mention is you can use any size pan, from a very small saucepan to a stockpot. The differences are the amount of oil needed to fill the pan appropriately and how many items can be fried at the same time. I customarily use a basic 2-qt/2-L saucepan with 3 to 4 in/7.5 to 10 cm of oil. Filling the pan about halfway provides oil in enough depth but not so much oil that it splashes over the sides.

02

DISKS OF CHILDHOOD PLEASURE. That's what my husband and I called cookies when our daughter was a toddler. She knew the word *cookie*, and we couldn't talk about cookies without piquing her interest in having one. So, we came up with a code phrase. Of course, she figured it out soon enough, but the name stuck for our family.

Cookies are also disks of adulthood pleasure. It's hard not to like cookies. And, it wouldn't be the winter holidays without them. They are the perfect treat for a busy season. You can make many batches in a short period of time and have them on hand for snacking, serving to visitors, bringing to cookie parties, and giving as gifts. Holiday cookies come in all flavors, shapes, and sizes. Some are simple, and some are complicated. Some are made with basic baking tools, while others require specialty equipment. I offer a range of cookie recipes, from easy to challenging, and from familiar to a bit unusual.

SPECULAAS

5 DOZEN COOKIES

These traditional Dutch cookies are often known as windmill cookies, because of the shape used in commercial products. In Holland, they are associated with St. Nicholas (the inspiration for Santa Claus) and are traditionally eaten on St. Nicholas's Eve, December 5. The origin of the name is debated. Some theorize that it comes from *speculum*, Latin for "mirror," referring to the design of the cookies being the mirror image of that on the mold. Or, it may derive from the Dutch *specerij*, or "spice." *Speculaas* cookies are very special to me. I never had the homemade version growing up, but my siblings and I loved the packaged cookies.

You can use any type of *speculaas* mold. The traditional ones are of St. Nicholas, or a windmill. You can also cut the dough with regular cookie cutters. The difference in shape between the *speculaas* and *springerle* cookies is that the *speculaas* cookies are cut into the shape of the design (say, a windmill) versus *springerle*, which are usually in the shape of a square, oval, or circle with an imprint of the design on top. Also, *speculaas* cookies are thinner and more crisp than *springerle*, which are thick and cakey. What distinguishes these cookies from other spice cookies is that they are made with a special spice mix called *speculaaskruiden*.

3 cups/420 g Jeanne's Gluten-Free All-Purpose Flour (page 17)

3½ tsp Speculaaskruiden (facing page)

¼ tsp salt

½ tsp baking powder

¾ cup/170 g unsalted butter, at room temperature

1½ cups/320 g packed dark brown sugar

1 extra-large egg, at room temperature

Tapioca flour for dusting

In a medium bowl, mix together the flour, *speculaaskruiden*, salt, and baking powder.

In a large bowl, using a spoon, stir together the butter and brown sugar until well combined. Add the egg and stir until combined. Add the flour mixture and stir until combined. The dough should be stiff but pliable. Divide the dough in half, shape each half into a disk, and wrap tightly in plastic wrap. Refrigerate for 30 to 60 minutes to meld the flavors and relax the dough.

Preheat the oven to 350°F/180°C/gas mark 4. Line two cookie sheets with parchment paper.

If using a *speculaas* mold, with a pastry brush, brush the mold with tapioca flour. Remove one dough disk from the refrigerator.

Place the dough between two sheets of waxed paper and roll out to ¼ in/6 mm thick. Peel off the top piece of waxed paper. Press the floured mold gently but firmly onto a section of the dough, pressing down as hard and as evenly as you can to be sure the imprint is made on the dough. Lift the mold from the dough. Carefully cut out the cookies with a pastry cutter or a sharp knife. Using a spatula, place on the prepared sheets, spacing them at least 1 in/2.5 cm apart. Make only a single imprint at a time—each time you press down on the mold, the dough moves, so if you try to press out more, you will distort the imprints. Repeat until all the dough is used, making sure to brush the mold with flour before each imprint.

If using cookie cutters, roll out the dough to ⅛ in/3 mm thick. Cut out as many shapes as possible and place on the prepared sheets, spacing them at least 1 in/2.5 cm apart.

Bake until the cookies are brown around the edges, 12 to 15 minutes. Remove to wire racks to cool completely. Let the sheets cool completely and repeat with the remaining dough.

Store in an airtight container at room temperature for up to 7 days.

SPECULAASKRUIDEN

4 tsp ground cinnamon
1 tsp ground cloves
1 tsp ground mace
½ tsp ground ginger
Pinch of ground white or black pepper
Pinch of ground cardamom
Pinch of ground coriander
Pinch of ground or crushed anise seeds
Pinch of freshly grated nutmeg

In a small bowl, stir together the cinnamon, cloves, mace, ginger, pepper, cardamom, coriander, anise, and nutmeg. Store in an airtight container for up to 3 months. The mix makes more than needed for the recipe. You can use the remainder for other things, like combining with brown sugar to top your morning oatmeal.

LEBKUCHEN

3 cups/420 g Jeanne's Gluten-Free All-Purpose Flour (page 17)

½ tsp baking soda

1 tsp ground cinnamon

1 tsp ground cloves

1 tsp freshly grated nutmeg

1 tsp ground allspice

½ cup/120 ml honey

½ cup/120 ml unsulphured molasses

½ cup/105 g packed dark brown sugar

1 tsp grated lemon zest

1 Tbsp freshly squeezed lemon juice

1 extra-large egg, at room temperature

½ cup/35 g ground almonds or hazelnuts

⅓ cup/45 g candied orange peel or candied citron (optional)

GLAZE

1 cup/115 g confectioners' sugar

2 Tbsp milk

I was lucky to have an *omi* ("granny" in German). She was my grandmother on my dad's side. She escaped from Germany just before the area where she lived was closed and called East Germany. When I was little, she resided in Queens, New York. Since we lived in California, every Christmas she sent us a huge box of assorted traditional German cookies, including highly spiced *lebkuchen*. I think of her whenever I bake these. *Lebkuchen* means "very sweet cakes," which makes sense because they are puffy, cakey cookies.

In a large bowl, mix together the flour, baking soda, cinnamon, cloves, nutmeg, and allspice.

In a medium saucepan, stir together the honey and molasses. Bring mixture to a boil over medium heat, then remove from the heat and let cool a bit. The mixture should be liquid enough so that it can easily be added to the other ingredients, so don't let it cool too much. Stir in the brown sugar, lemon zest, and lemon juice. Quickly whisk in the egg, whisking constantly so that the egg doesn't cook.

Add the molasses mixture to the flour mixture and stir to combine. Stir in the nuts and the candied orange peel (if using). Cover the bowl tightly with plastic wrap and refrigerate for 1 hour, or up to 3 days.

Preheat the oven to 350°F/180°C/gas mark 4. Line two cookie sheets with parchment paper.

Remove the dough from the refrigerator. The dough will be extremely stiff and sticky. Pull off 1-Tbsp pieces and roll into balls between your hands. (If the dough is too sticky, wet your hands slightly). Place the balls on the prepared sheets, spacing them about 2 in/5 cm apart. After each sheet is filled, place a piece of waxed paper over the dough balls and, using the bottom of a glass, press each dough ball to form a disk ¼ in/6 mm thick. Gently and carefully peel off the waxed paper. The dough is extremely sticky, but you should be able to peel off the paper if you do it slowly.

Bake for about 15 minutes. To test for doneness, very lightly press the top of a cookie with a finger. If it is done, the imprint of your finger should not remain. Remove the cookies to wire racks to cool slightly. Let the sheets cool completely and repeat with the remaining dough.

WHILE THE COOKIES ARE COOLING, MAKE THE GLAZE / Sift the confectioners' sugar into a small bowl. Add the milk and whisk to combine. The mixture will be thick but still liquid. Place cookie sheets under the wire racks of cookies. Dip the top of each warm cookie in the glaze and, over the bowl, tip the cookie to one side and then the other to allow the extra glaze to drip off. Place the glazed cookies back on the racks to allow the glaze to set. If you like, leave some cookies plain. They are delicious both ways!

Store in an airtight container at room temperature for up to 2 weeks.

PFEFFERNUESSE

Pfeffernuesse, "pepper nuts" in German, are especially popular during the Christmas season. They are called pepper nuts because of their spiciness. The dough contains pepper, sometimes black, sometimes white. I give you a choice. As with many spice cookies, these can be allowed to mellow for a few days after baking.

3 cups/420 g Jeanne's Gluten-Free All-Purpose Flour (page 17)

½ tsp baking soda

1 tsp finely ground black or white pepper

½ tsp ground cinnamon

¼ tsp ground ginger

¼ tsp ground cloves

¼ tsp ground cardamom

½ tsp ground allspice

½ tsp grated lemon zest

½ cup/115 g unsalted butter, at room temperature

⅔ cup/140 g packed dark brown sugar

¼ cup/60 ml unsulphured molasses

1 tsp pure vanilla extract

2 extra-large eggs, at room temperature

¾ cup/85 g confectioners' sugar

Preheat the oven to 350°F/180°C/gas mark 4. Line two cookie sheets with parchment paper.

In a small bowl, mix together the flour, baking soda, pepper, cinnamon, ginger, cloves, cardamom, allspice, and lemon zest.

In a large bowl, using a hand mixer on medium-high speed, beat the butter until fluffy, about 1 minute. Add the brown sugar, molasses, and vanilla, and beat for 1 minute. Reduce the speed to medium and add the eggs, one at a time, beating after each addition. Increase the speed to medium-high and beat for 1 minute. Reduce the speed to low, add the flour mixture, and beat until just combined. The dough will be thick.

Scoop up 1-Tbsp pieces of dough and roll into balls with your hands. (If the dough is too sticky, wet your hands slightly.) Place the balls on the prepared sheets, spacing them 2 in/5 cm apart.

Bake until the cookies are firm, 15 to 20 minutes. Remove the cookies to wire racks to cool completely. Let the sheets cool completely and repeat with the remaining dough.

Place the confectioners' sugar in a medium bowl. Carefully roll each cookie in the sugar until coated. You may also leave some uncoated.

Store in an airtight container at room temperature for up to 2 weeks.

SPRINGERLE

4 cups/560 g Jeanne's Gluten-Free All-Purpose Flour (page 17), plus more for kneading

¼ tsp salt

½ tsp baking powder

3 extra-large eggs, at room temperature

3 cups/340 g confectioners' sugar

¼ cup/55 g unsalted butter, at room temperature

¼ tsp pure vanilla extract

¼ tsp anise oil or extract

¼ tsp lemon oil or extract

1 Tbsp milk

Tapioca flour for dusting

ABOUT 40 COOKIES These delicate, cakey German cookies have been around, some say, for hundreds of years. The name *springerle* comes from an old German word meaning " jumping horse" or "little knight," which probably refers to the original shapes of the molds. *Springerle* molds are amazingly beautiful and detailed. Each is a work of art, and I would buy every one if I had the budget. The mold I used for this recipe makes cookies that measure about 1½ by 1¾ in/4 by 4.5 cm. The cookies are traditionally flavored with anise and lemon oils. If you want a milder taste, use the corresponding extracts.

Making the cookies takes 2 days. The first day, you prepare the dough and cut out the cookies. The next day, you bake them.

Line two cookie sheets with parchment paper.

In a medium bowl, mix together the 4 cups/ 560 g flour, salt, and baking powder.

In the bowl of a stand mixer fitted with the whisk attachment, beat the eggs on medium-high speed until thick and light yellow, about 20 minutes. Slowly add the confectioners' sugar, a little at a time, beating after each addition. Continue to beat until smooth. Add the butter and beat until creamy, about 2 minutes. Add the vanilla, anise oil, and lemon oil and beat until combined. Add the milk, beating until combined.

Change to the paddle attachment. Add the flour mixture a little at a time and beat on medium-low speed until combined. The dough will be stiff.

Turn out the dough onto a board generously dusted with all-purpose flour mix. Knead the dough, incorporating more flour, until the dough is quite stiff and will retain the imprint of the *springerle* mold. (The dough is ready when it is no longer sticky. The humidity in your kitchen will determine how much more flour will be needed.)

Dust your rolling surface and your rolling pin with tapioca flour. With a pastry brush, brush the insides of the mold well with tapioca flour.

Roll out the dough to about ½ in/12 mm thick (no thinner). Firmly and carefully press the mold onto the dough, making a good impression—you will need to press hard and evenly around all parts of the mold. Remove the mold by lifting it straight up, so you don't alter the impression as the mold disengages from the dough. Carefully cut out the cookies with a pastry cutter, a sharp knife, or a cookie cutter that is the same shape as your mold. Using a spatula, place the cookies on the prepared sheets, spacing them ½ in/12 mm apart. Only imprint and cut one mold at a time. If you do more, all the dough will move, and the previously imprinted designs will be distorted. Repeat until all the dough is used.

CONTINUED /

Let the cookies dry, uncovered, at room temperature, for 12 to 24 hours. The drying period helps form a film on the top that sets the design when the cookies are baked. When you are ready to bake the cookies, check the bottom of a cookie to make sure it is still moist. This will help anchor the cookies to the parchment paper and allow them to rise.

Preheat the oven to 300°F/150°C/gas mark 2 for cookies measuring 2½ in/6 mm or smaller or to 325°F/165°C/gas mark 3 for cookies measuring 3 in/7.5 cm or larger.

Bake until the cookies are barely brown on the bottom, 10 to 25 minutes, depending on the size. The cookies should remain white on top—do not gauge doneness by the tops browning. When you take a cookie from the sheet, look at the bottom. When it is done, there should be cracking along the bottom rising points—kind of like an inner square with lines going to each corner or, for circles, an inner circle. Remove the cookies to wire racks to cool completely.

Store in an airtight container. Traditionally, *springerle* are baked several weeks before Christmas and are allowed to "age" in the container at room temperature to mellow the anise taste. In our family, we eat some of the cookies soon after baking and others later after they have aged.

PEPPARKAKOR

These traditional Christmas gingersnaps from Sweden are among the many gingerbread-type cookies that abound during this season. The name translates to "spicy cookie." This recipe is adapted from one sent to me by my friend Emily. It's a family recipe from her Swedish grandmother, and Emily and her kids make the cookies every year. One of the wonderful things about the recipe is its versatility. These cookies are cut out with shapes, the most traditional being hearts and people. I like the aroma that fills the house when I bake these cookies.

3 cups/420 g Jeanne's Gluten-Free All-Purpose Flour (page 17)

3 tsp ground ginger

2 tsp ground cinnamon

2 tsp ground cloves

½ tsp salt

1 tsp baking soda

1 cup/225 g unsalted butter, at room temperature

1 cup/200 g granulated sugar

½ cup/120 ml unsulphured molasses

½ cup/60 g finely chopped almonds (optional)

In a small bowl, mix together the flour, ginger, cinnamon, cloves, salt, and baking soda.

In the bowl of a stand mixer fitted with the paddle attachment, beat the butter and sugar on medium-high speed until light and fluffy, about 2 minutes. Add the molasses and beat until combined. Add the flour mixture and stir by hand until all the ingredients are combined. The dough will be stiff. Add the nuts (if using) and mix in well by hand.

Divide the dough into three pieces, shape each into a disk, and wrap tightly in plastic wrap. Refrigerate until firm, for at least 1 hour, or up to 3 days.

Preheat the oven to 350°F/180°C/gas mark 4. Line two cookie sheets with parchment paper.

Remove one dough disk from the refrigerator, place between two sheets of waxed paper, and roll to ⅛ in/3 mm thick. Using 2 ½-in/6.5-cm cookie cutters, cut as many shapes as possible. Using a spatula, place the cutouts on the prepared sheets, spacing them at least 1 in/2.5 cm apart. The cookies will puff during baking. Roll out the dough scraps and repeat the process. The dough is best cut when it is firm, so you may have to return it to the refrigerator before cutting more shapes.

Bake until the cookies are darker in color (the dough is already very dark), 12 to 14 minutes. Watch them carefully so that they do not burn. Remove to wire racks to cool. The cookies will become crisp as they cool. Let the sheets cool completely and repeat with the remaining dough.

Store in an airtight container at room temperature for up to 1 week. The cookies may be frozen for up to 6 weeks.

RUGELACH

2 cups/280 g Jeanne's Gluten-Free All-Purpose Flour (page 17)

Pinch of salt

8 oz/225 g cool but not cold cream cheese, cut into 1-in/2.5-cm cubes

1 cup/225 g cool but not cold unsalted butter, cut into 1-in/2.5-cm cubes

2 Tbsp granulated sugar

Tapioca flour for dusting

JAM FILLING

½ cup/120 ml smooth jam of your choice

½ cup/80 g mini semisweet chocolate chips

CURRANT-NUT FILLING

¼ cup/55 g packed dark brown sugar

¼ tsp ground cinnamon

½ cup/60 g dried currants

½ cup/60 g chopped pecans, walnuts, or hazelnuts

1 extra-large egg beaten with 1 Tbsp water, for egg wash (optional)

2 DOZEN COOKIES The word *rugelach* means "little twists" in Yiddish. Rugelach, somewhat resembling mini croissants, are traditional filled and rolled cookies often eaten during Hanukkah in honor of Judith. Her story relates to the military struggle that led to the events of Hanukkah. In short, Judith was a widow who saved her village from the Assyrian general Holofernes. She snuck into his camp, ingratiated herself to him so he would trust her, and then served him extremely salty cheese. The cheese made him so thirsty that he drank too much wine and became drunk. Taking advantage of the situation, Judith decapitated him with his own dagger. His soldiers, having no leader, dispersed, and the Israelites were saved. Thus, rugelach and other foods made from dairy honor the cheese in the story. These cookies have a rich cream cheese crust that envelops a sweet filling—usually containing jam and/or nuts, dried fruit, or chocolate chips. To me, these taste a bit like filled croissants—they are light, flaky, and decadent!

I give two options for the filling. You can use any combination of the fillings, or spread some jam (one that's not too chunky) on the dough and sprinkle with pecans. The sky's the limit as far as what you can use to fill the cookies.

In a small bowl, mix together the flour and salt.

In the bowl of a stand mixer fitted with the paddle attachment, beat the cream cheese on medium speed until fluffy, about 2 minutes. Add the butter and beat until light and fluffy, about 2 minutes. Add the granulated sugar and mix to combine. Add the flour mixture and beat until the dough comes together in a lump. By this time, your mixer will be working hard.

Using your hands, gather the lump of dough and bring it together into a smooth, cohesive mass. Divide the dough in half and shape each half into a disk. You may use the dough immediately (it should still be cold). Or, wrap each disk tightly in plastic wrap and refrigerate for up to 3 days or freeze for up to 6 months (defrost by transferring the dough

to the refrigerator 24 hours before using). If using the dough right away, wrap a disk with plastic wrap and refrigerate while you work with the other disk.

Preheat the oven to 375°F/190°C/gas mark 5. Line a cookie sheet with parchment paper.

Sprinkle your rolling surface and your rolling pin with tapioca flour. Place the dough disk in the middle of the surface and sprinkle with a little tapioca flour. You will be rolling the dough into a circle and cutting it into wedges—so take care during the rolling process. Give the dough a roll. Gently grab the dough by one side, lift it, and give it a quarter turn. Roll again. Lift and turn. Keep doing this until you have a nicely shaped circle of dough roughly 12 in/30.5 cm in

diameter and ⅛ in/3 mm thick (no thicker). If the dough cracks around the edges, just press the dough together and keep going. The ideal temperature for the dough when rolling is cool but not too hard and cold. Alternatively, you don't want it to be warm and sweating.

IF USING THE JAM FILLING / Evenly spread ¼ cup/60 ml of the jam on the circle of dough, leaving a 1-in/2.5-cm border uncovered around the edges. Cut the dough into 12 equal wedges with a pastry cutter or a sharp knife. I recommend making an initial cut from top to bottom, and then another cut from side to side, dividing the circle into equal quarters. Then, cut 3 equal wedges from each quarter. After you've cut the dough, carefully sprinkle on ¼ cup/40 g of the chocolate chips, again leaving a 1-in/2.5-cm border around the edges.

IF USING THE CURRANT-NUT FILLING / Combine the brown sugar, cinnamon, currants, and nuts in a small bowl. Cut the dough into 12 equal wedges with a pastry cutter or a sharp knife. I recommend making an initial cut from top to bottom, and then another cut from side to side, dividing the circle into equal quarters. Then, cut 3 equal wedges from each quarter. Carefully sprinkle half of the filling on the dough, leaving a 1-in/2.5-cm border around the edges. Take the rolling pin and very carefully use it to squish the filling into the dough a bit. What I do is tap the pin all over the dough. This helps the filling adhere to the dough and not fall off so much when rolling the dough.

Now you're ready to roll the dough into logs. Pull out a wedge from the dough round. Starting from the wide end, slowly and carefully roll the dough around the filling until you reach the point of the wedge. The dough may crack a bit—just smooth it over and keep going. Arrange the logs on the prepared sheet, placing the side with the point down and spacing the logs about 1½ in/4 cm apart. This will help the logs retain their rolled shape during baking. Using a pastry brush, lightly brush each cookie with some of the egg wash (if using).

Bake until the cookies are a uniform golden brown, 25 to 30 minutes. Immediately remove to wire racks to cool completely so the cookies don't stick to the parchment paper with any filling that might have leaked out. Let the sheet cool completely and repeat with the remaining dough and fillings.

Store at room temperature in an airtight container for up to 3 days.

BENNE COOKIES

6 DOZEN COOKIES

Benne is the Bantu word for "sesame seeds," which were brought from Africa to the United States in the eighteenth century. Bantu is a family that comprises many different languages across Africa, including Zulu and Swahili. *Bantu* itself means "the people." My family adores these cookies. They are unexpectedly delicious as a sweet cookie. The toasted sesame seeds mixed with the butter and sugar create a rich flavor not usually associated with sesame seeds. And they are especially appropriate for Kwanzaa celebrations because of the seeds' connection to Africa.

1 cup/140 g sesame seeds

1 cup/140 g Jeanne's Gluten-Free All-Purpose Flour (page 17)

½ tsp baking powder

¼ tsp salt

¾ cup/170 g unsalted butter, at room temperature

1½ cups/320 g packed dark brown sugar

1 extra-large egg, at room temperature

1 tsp pure vanilla extract

Preheat the oven to 375°F/190°C/gas mark 5.

Scatter the sesame seeds on an ungreased cookie sheet. Toast until the seeds are light brown, 10 to 12 minutes. Stir the seeds a couple of times while they toast to make sure they brown evenly. Watch so that they do not burn. Pour the toasted seeds into a bowl and let cool.

Line two cookie sheets with parchment paper.

In a small bowl, mix together the flour, baking powder, and salt.

In a large bowl, using a spoon, stir together the butter and brown sugar until smooth. Add the egg and beat with the spoon until fully incorporated. Add the vanilla and stir to combine. Add the sesame seeds and mix to combine. Add the flour mixture and stir to combine.

Drop the dough by heaping teaspoons onto the prepared sheets, spacing them about 1 in/2.5 cm apart—they will spread. Bake until the cookies are brown on the edges, 6 to 8 minutes. Let cool on the sheets for 2 minutes, then remove to wire racks to cool completely. Let the sheets cool completely and repeat with the remaining dough.

Store in an airtight container at room temperature for up to 5 days.

FORTUNE COOKIES

ABOUT 30 COOKIES Fortune cookies are so much fun to make and to eat. The cookie is basically a French *tuile*, meaning "tile," named after the roof tiles of French country houses that the cookies supposedly resemble. The flat, crispy, and delicate cookies are quite simple to make—you just need patience to get them folded right. I love to serve the cookies to friends and family because no one ever prepares homemade fortune cookies and everyone is always impressed! Offering them at your New Year's Eve party provides your guests with delicious predictions for the upcoming year.

Butter for greasing (optional)

1 egg white

¼ cup/50 g granulated sugar

1 Tbsp neutral-flavored oil such as rice bran or canola

2 Tbsp water, at room temperature

½ tsp pure vanilla extract

½ tsp grated orange zest

¼ cup/35 g Jeanne's Gluten-Free All-Purpose Flour (page 17)

Pinch of salt

Please read through entire recipe before starting so you understand the process. Once you begin, you need to work quickly. Have at the ready a plate for folding the baked cookies, a mug on which to bend the cookies into shape, and a muffin pan in which to cool the shaped cookies. Before you make the cookies, you can enjoy coming up with fortunes. You want to write them on paper strips about 3 in/7.5 cm long and ½ in/12 mm wide. You will need 30.

Preheat the oven to 350°F/180°C/gas mark 4. Line a cookie sheet with a Silpat silicone mat or grease very well with butter (the cookie batter is extremely sticky). If you grease the sheet, you will need to regrease it each time you bake a batch of cookies.

In a small bowl, whisk the egg white until foamy, about 30 seconds. Add the sugar and whisk for 10 seconds. Add the oil and the water and whisk until combined. Add the vanilla and orange zest and whisk until combined. Add the flour and the salt and whisk until the mixture is smooth.

Spoon the batter by teaspoonfuls onto the prepared sheet. Smooth out the batter by moving the back of the spoon on the batter in an increasing circle, until the circle is about 3 in/7.5 cm in diameter (no larger). The batter will look uneven, with some spots having more batter than others. Just try to make it as even as you can. Repeat to make another circle of batter, spacing it at least 2 in/5 cm from the first circle. You want to start by making two cookies at a time because folding the baked cookies needs to happen quickly. After you get the hang of it, you can move up to baking four cookies at a time.

Bake until the cookies are browned at the edges, 10 to 12 minutes. (Note that the baking times will vary depending on the batter temperature and conditions in your kitchen.) Working quickly, carefully lift a cookie from the sheet with a spatula, place it bottom up on the plate, put a fortune in the middle, and fold the cookie in half. Then pick up the cookie by the pointy ends with your thumbs and

CONTINUED /

forefingers and press the middle of the folded edge on the rim of the mug, bringing the ends downward so they touch either side of the mug to create a U shape. The cookie will look like a fan. Place the cookie in a muffin cup so that it retains its shape until it cools. Working quickly, repeat with the other cookie.

After the cookies have cooled in the muffin pan for a few minutes, remove them to a wire rack to cool completely. The muffin cups encourage moisture to build up on the cookies due to their retained warmth, and the cookies won't be completely crisp in the center unless they are aired out a bit.

Repeat the process until you've used all the batter. After baking each batch, let the cookie sheet cool to the touch and scrape off any bits of cookie that have built up on the spatula.

The cookies are usually best the day you make them but can be stored in an airtight container at room temperature for up to 1 week. To recrisp the cookies, place in an unlined muffin pan in a preheated 250°F/120°C/gas mark ½ oven for 10 minutes. Let cool in the pan until crisp, then remove to a wire rack to cool completely.

MEXICAN
WEDDING COOKIES

2 cups/280 g Jeanne's Gluten-
Free All-Purpose Flour (page 17)

½ tsp salt

1 cup/225 g unsalted butter,
at room temperature

2 cups/225 g confectioners' sugar,
sifted

2 tsp pure vanilla extract

1 cup/120 g pecans or walnuts,
toasted and coarsely ground or
chopped

⅛ tsp cinnamon (optional)

ABOUT 4 DOZEN COOKIES These cookies, resembling little, light, crunchy cakes, are descendants of medieval Arab cuisine, whose confections using sugar, butter, and nuts were made for celebratory occasions. They were adopted by Europeans at some point and appeared at tea ceremonies, weddings, and Christmas. The cookies that we eat today were popularly known as Russian tea cakes in the late nineteenth and early twentieth centuries because, presumably, they were served with tea. Their association with special events continued, and around the 1950s, versions of the cookies were called Mexican wedding cookies. Whatever their name, they are easily one of the simplest cookies to make—basically a butter cookie with ground nuts. They are lighter than air because of the confectioners' sugar, and they almost melt in your mouth. I used to make a version of the cookies when I was young—they were among my favorite cookies—and I have never stopped.

In a small bowl, mix together the flour and salt.

In the bowl of a stand mixer fitted with the paddle attachment, beat the butter on medium-high speed until light and fluffy, about 2 minutes. Add ½ cup/55 g of the confectioners' sugar and beat for 2 minutes. Add the vanilla and beat on low speed until combined. Add the flour mixture and beat until just combined. Add the nuts and continue to beat on low speed until combined.

Divide the dough in half. Form each half into a ball and wrap tightly in plastic wrap. Refrigerate until firm, about 30 minutes, or for up to 3 days.

Preheat the oven to 350°F/180°C/gas mark 4. Line two cookie sheets with parchment paper.

Place the remaining 1½ cups/170 g sugar in a medium bowl. Add the cinnamon (if using) and mix to combine.

Remove one dough ball from the refrigerator. Pull off 1-Tbsp chunks of dough and roll into balls with your hands. Place the balls on the prepared sheets, spacing them about ½ in/12 mm apart. Work quickly—you don't want the dough to warm up too much. Bake until the cookies are just golden brown on top, 18 to 20 minutes. Let cool on the cookie sheets for about 5 minutes. Gently toss each cookie in the sugar until completely coated. Place the coated cookies on wire racks to cool completely. Let the sheets cool completely and repeat with the remaining dough.

Store in an airtight container at room temperature for up to 3 days. (It is nice to reserve the remaining sugar in an airtight container to sprinkle on the cookies just before serving—to make sure the stored cookies are well coated.)

SPRITZ COOKIES

SPRITZ COOKIES

ABOUT 8 DOZEN COOKIES Also called pressed butter cookies, *spritz* are the perfect holiday cookie. They are simple to make with a cookie press (see page 27), pretty to look at, and delicious to eat. This recipe makes about eight dozen. Yes, you read that right—eight dozen. And the cookies are quick to prepare and ideal for giving as gifts or bringing to cookie parties. You can serve the baked cookies plain or decorate them any number of ways. I like to slather melted chocolate between two cookies for an elegant sandwich cookie. It's also fun to drizzle melted chocolate over the tops. You can also sprinkle the cookies with colored sugar or decorate them with royal icing (see page 59).

2¼ cups/315 g Jeanne's Gluten-Free All-Purpose Flour (page 17)

¼ tsp salt

1 cup/225 g unsalted butter, at room temperature

½ cup/100 g granulated sugar

1 extra-large egg, plus egg yolk, at room temperature

¾ tsp pure vanilla extract

Colored sugar for sprinkling (optional)

1 cup/170 g semisweet chocolate chips (optional)

Preheat the oven to 350°F/180°C/gas mark 4. Have ready two ungreased cookie sheets.

In a small bowl, mix together the flour and salt.

In the bowl of a stand mixer fitted with the paddle attachment, beat the butter on medium speed until light, about 1 minute. Add the granulated sugar and beat for 1 minute. Add the whole egg and egg yolk and beat for 1 minute. Add the vanilla and beat until combined. Reduce the speed to low, add the flour mixture, and beat until combined.

Here comes the fun part. Prepare your cookie press by placing the plunger on the tube part and turn to lock. Lift the plunger until it's all the way at the top. Then fill the tube with the dough from the bottom opening. Fit the disk of your choice into the bottom ring and screw on tightly. Now press the gun part (it will click each time you press the handle) until you see dough just pushing against the disk at the bottom.

Now you're ready to press out dough. Place the end of the press firmly and evenly against a cookie sheet and press once on the gun. Lift the press. If the dough was adequately pressed against the disk, you should have a nice cookie shape on the sheet. If dough came out but did not stick, or if the shape is wonky, pick up the dough and put it back into the bowl (I told you this would be easy). Press out enough cookies to cover the cookie sheets, spacing them about 1½ in/4 cm apart. Lightly sprinkle with colored sugar (if using). I usually sprinkle some with colored sugar and leave some plain.

Bake until the cookies are light brown on the bottoms, 13 to 15 minutes. Remove to wire racks to cool completely. Repeat the process with the remaining dough, allowing the cookie sheets to cool completely. If the dough starts to seem too squishy to make defined shapes, refrigerate it for a few minutes.

If you like melt the chocolate chips in a small saucepan over extremely low heat until

CONTINUED /

just barely melted. Watch carefully to prevent burning. Remove from the heat and whisk until smooth. Line a cookie sheet with waxed paper. With a butter knife, spread a bit of melted chocolate on the bottoms of some of the cookies and press the cookies, chocolate-side down, onto the waxed paper. For sandwich cookies, spread melted chocolate on the bottom of a cookie and press the bottom of another cookie of the same shape onto the chocolate. Or drizzle melted chocolate on top of the shapes. Be creative! Let the cookies sit for about 1 hour to let the chocolate set.

Store in an airtight container, with waxed paper between the layers, at room temperature for up to 7 days.

SHORTBREAD COOKIES

12 TO 16 WEDGES

¾ cup/170 g unsalted butter, cut into smaller pieces, plus more for greasing the pan

1¾ cup/245 g Jeanne's Gluten-Free All-Purpose Flour (page 17)

Pinch of salt

½ cup/100 g granulated sugar

½ tsp pure vanilla extract

Originating in Scotland, shortbread was among the first types of butter cookie. It was initially made with just three ingredients: flour, butter, and sugar. Over the years, bakers have added flavorings, like salt and vanilla. Shortbread is traditionally served on the Scottish holiday Hogmanay, a New Year's Eve celebration that lasts from the evening of December 31 through January 2. The origin of the word is much debated, but it seems to have come from an old French word for a gift given at New Year's or for New Year's itself. Shortbread cookies are delicate—they are crumbly, taste of butter and vanilla, and will melt in your mouth.

Preheat the oven to 350°F/180°C/gas mark 4. Grease a 9-in/23-cm pie pan with butter.

In the bowl of a stand mixer fitted with the paddle attachment, beat the flour, salt, butter, sugar, and vanilla on medium until the mixture looks like wet sand (this may take a few minutes).

Turn out the dough into the prepared pie pan. (It will pour like wet sand.) Carefully press the dough into the pie pan. The dough should cover the bottom of the pan and not go up the sides. With a sharp knife, cut 12 to 16 equal wedges. I recommend making an initial cut from top to bottom, and then another cut from side to side, dividing the circle into equal quarters. Then, cut 3 to 4 equal wedges from each quarter. After you've cut the dough, prick it all over with the tines of a fork.

Bake until the edges begin to brown, about 40 minutes. Remove from the oven and place the pan on a wire rack to cool. With a sharp knife, carefully recut the cookie wedges. Let the cookies cool completely.

Store in an airtight container at room temperature for up to 3 days, or in the refrigerator for up to 7 days.

CANDY CANE COOKIES

ABOUT 40 COOKIES These cookies are a pretty (and delicious) addition to a cookie plate. They are fashioned of cylinders of pink and white dough that are twisted together and shaped to look like candy canes. Even though the process looks somewhat difficult, making the cookies is quite easy—it takes time because you need to go slow and steady. You have the option of flavoring the cookies with peppermint extract to add a minty kick.

2½ cups/350 g Jeanne's Gluten-Free All-Purpose Flour (page 17)

1 tsp salt

1 cup/225 g unsalted butter, at room temperature

1 cup/115 g confectioners' sugar

1 extra-large egg

1 tsp pure vanilla extract

½ tsp peppermint extract (optional)

5 or 6 drops of red food coloring, or as needed

Tapioca flour for dusting

In a small bowl, mix together the flour and salt.

In the bowl of a stand mixer fitted with the paddle attachment, beat the butter on medium speed for 1 minute. Add the confectioners' sugar and beat for 1 minute. Add the egg and beat for 2 minutes (if the mixture looks curdled, it means that the butter is a bit too cold to combine with the egg. This will be rectified when you add the flour.) Add the vanilla and beat until combined. Reduce the speed to low, add the flour mixture, and beat until combined and the dough comes together. Keep beating until the last bits of flour at the bottom of the bowl are incorporated into the dough.

Divide the dough in half. Leave half in the bowl and wrap the other half in plastic wrap. To the dough in the bowl, add the peppermint extract (if using). Add the food coloring and, with the back of a spoon, mix until the color is spread equally throughout the dough. The dough will be pinkish, and it will be quite soft. Wrap the pink dough in plastic wrap, and refrigerate both portions of dough until firm, about 2 hours.

Line two large serving trays or other large, flat trays with waxed paper. These will be holding trays for the rolled-out dough.

Place a piece of waxed paper on your rolling surface. Put a large pinch of tapioca flour on one side of the waxed paper for dipping the dough as needed. Remove the white dough from the refrigerator. Scoop out a 1-tsp portion of the dough and roll into a ball with your hands. It will be about the size of a marble. Then roll each ball into a skinny, even cylinder about 5 in/12 cm long. I do this by dipping the ball into the tapioca flour on all sides and rolling it between my palms (not my fingers) to about 3 in/7.5 cm long. I place the cylinder on the waxed paper and roll it out to the full length. Arrange the cylinders on a prepared tray. Repeat with the remaining dough. You should have about 40 cylinders. You need to work quickly, because the dough starts to become floppy when it's too warm. If this happens, refrigerate the dough to firm it up a bit. Cover the tray with plastic wrap and refrigerate.

CONTINUED /

Repeat the process with the tinted dough to make the same amount of cylinders, placing them on a prepared tray and refrigerating them until firm but not stiff or rock hard.

Remove the dough cylinders from the refrigerator. Place a white cylinder and a tinted cylinder side by side on the rolling surface. Twist the cylinders together, then pinch at both ends. Make a curve at one end to form the hook of the cane. If the cylinders break, just pinch them together. Place the canes on the waxed paper–lined trays. Return to the refrigerator to firm up, about 15 minutes.

Preheat the oven to 350°F/180°C/gas mark 4. Line two cookie sheets with parchment paper.

Arrange the canes on the prepared sheets, spacing them about 1 in/2.5 cm apart. Return any remaining canes to the refrigerator. Bake until the cookies are slightly browned on the tips and the bottoms, 15 to 18 minutes. Let cool on the sheets for about 5 minutes, then remove to wire racks to cool completely. Let the sheets cool completely and bake the remaining canes.

These cookies are somewhat fragile because of their shape—handle them carefully! Store in an airtight container at room temperature for up to 5 days.

CUTOUT COOKIES

ABOUT 30 COOKIES Cutout cookies are a must for the holiday season. The wonderful thing about this dough is that it can be cut into any shape or size that a particular holiday requires. I make the dough year-round and use cookie cutters that suit the occasion. The cookies are fun to decorate. When my daughter was a toddler, we painted the icing on the cookies instead of piping it. Painting the cookies was so much easier. Now that she is older, it is a wonderful way for both of us to get creative when decorating the cookies. Each cookie can be a masterpiece.

2 cups / 280 g Jeanne's Gluten-Free All-Purpose Flour (page 17)

1½ tsp baking powder

¼ tsp salt

½ cup / 115 g unsalted butter, at room temperature

1 cup / 200 g granulated sugar

1 extra-large egg, at room temperature

1 tsp pure vanilla extract

½ tsp grated lemon or orange zest (optional)

Tapioca flour for dusting

Colored sugar for decorating (optional)

ICING

2 cups / 225 g confectioners' sugar, sifted

1 tsp pure vanilla extract

4 to 6 Tbsp heavy cream, or more if needed

Food coloring in various colors (optional)

In a medium bowl, mix together the flour, baking powder, and salt.

In a large bowl, using a hand mixer on medium-high speed, beat the butter until light and fluffy, about 2 minutes. Add the granulated sugar and beat for 1 minute. Add the egg and beat for 1 minute. Add the vanilla and beat to combine. Add the lemon zest (if using). Add the flour mixture and beat until combined.

Divide the dough in half, shape each half into a disk, and wrap tightly in plastic wrap. Refrigerate until firm, about 30 minutes, or for up to 3 days.

Preheat the oven to 375°F/190°C/gas mark 5. Line two cookie sheets with parchment paper.

Remove one dough disk from the refrigerator. If the dough is rock hard, let it warm up a bit. Place the dough between two pieces of waxed paper and roll to ⅛ in/3 mm thick. Using cookie cutters dipped in tapioca flour, cut out as many shapes as possible. Using a spatula, place the cutouts on the prepared sheets, spacing them at least 1 in/2.5 cm apart. Roll out the dough scraps and repeat the process until all the dough is used or the cookie sheets are full. The dough is best cut

when it is firm, so you may have to return it to the refrigerator before cutting more shapes.

Sprinkle the shapes with colored sugar (if desired or leave them plain and decorate with icing after baking). Bake until the edges of the cookies are lightly browned, 8 to 10 minutes. Let cool on the cookie sheets for about 2 minutes, then remove to wire racks to cool completely. Let the sheets cool completely and repeat with the remaining dough.

WHILE THE COOKIES ARE COOLING, MAKE THE ICING / Place the confectioners' sugar in a large bowl. Add the vanilla and 4 Tbsp of the cream. Whisk until all the ingredients are combined and smooth. If desired, add more cream to make the icing thinner. If you want to color the icing, divide it among small bowls and tint each bowl of icing with a different food coloring. Using a small paintbrush per color, decorate the cookies. Place the decorated cookies on the wire racks to let the icing set.

Store the cookies in an airtight container, between layers of waxed paper, at room temperature for up to 5 days or in the refrigerator for up to 2 weeks.

THUMBPRINT COOKIES

5 DOZEN COOKIES

The inspiration for this recipe comes from one of my all-time favorite cookie cookbook authors, Nancy Baggett. It turns out that she has a family member who is gluten intolerant. We "met" when she wrote me that she used my version of her recipe to make these beloved cookies for her family. Thumbprint cookies are some of the easiest and most fun cookies to prepare—especially with children. Kids like that they are allowed (nay, encouraged!) to touch the dough and squish it in the middle. The cookies give me an excuse to break out my homemade jam. In addition to being a baker, I am an avid canner and always have many jams in my pantry. Go wild and use all your favorite jams for a stained-glass effect on the serving tray. You can save the egg whites to make Chocolate Chip Meringues (page 61).

3½ cups/490 g Jeanne's Gluten-Free All-Purpose Flour (page 17)

¼ tsp salt

1½ cups/340 g unsalted butter, slightly softened

1 cup/200 g granulated sugar

3 egg yolks

2 tsp pure vanilla extract

1 cup/240 ml jam of your choice

Preheat the oven to 375°F/190°C/gas mark 5. Line two cookie sheets with parchment paper.

In a small bowl, mix together the flour and salt.

In the bowl of a stand mixer fitted with the paddle attachment, beat the butter on medium speed until light and fluffy, about 1 minute. Add the sugar and beat for 1 minute. Add the egg yolks, one at a time, beating after each addition. Add the vanilla and beat to combine. Add the flour mixture and beat until combined.

Scoop out 1-Tbsp pieces of dough and roll into balls with your hands. Place the balls on the prepared sheets, spacing them 1½ to 2 in/4 to 5 cm apart. With a finger, make a deep indentation in the center of each ball.

Bake until the cookies just begin to brown, about 9 minutes. Remove from the oven and fill each indentation with a heaping ½ tsp jam. Continue to bake until the jam starts to melt and the bottoms of the cookies are golden brown, about 9 minutes longer. Remove to wire racks to cool completely. Let the sheets cool completely and repeat with the remaining dough.

Store in an airtight container at room temperature for up to 5 days.

GINGERBREAD
COOKIES

4 DOZEN MEDIUM COOKIES Gingerbread cookies are the quintessential Christmas cookie. This recipe calls for the same dough prepared for the Gingerbread House. You can use cookie cutters to create any shapes you want. I have to say that you should make at least a few gingerbread men and women.

4½ cups/630 g Jeanne's Gluten-Free All-Purpose Flour (page 17)

1 tsp salt

1 tsp baking soda

1 tsp freshly ground nutmeg

1 Tbsp ground ginger

1 cup/225 g unsalted butter

1 cup/200 g granulated sugar

1 cup/240 ml unsulphured molasses

ROYAL ICING

3 egg whites

4 cups/450 g confectioners' sugar, plus more if needed

½ tsp cream of tartar

In a large bowl, mix together the flour, salt, baking soda, nutmeg, and ginger.

In a heavy saucepan over medium-low heat, melt the butter. Add the granulated sugar and molasses and stir until the sugar has dissolved completely.

Carefully pour the sugar mixture into the bowl of a stand mixer fitted with the paddle attachment. Add the flour mixture and beat on low speed for several seconds until combined. The dough will be stiff and oily. Divide the dough into three fairly equal pieces, wrap tightly in plastic wrap, and refrigerate until firm, about 1 hour.

Preheat the oven to 375°F/190°C/gas mark 5. Line two cookie sheets with parchment paper.

Remove one piece of dough from the refrigerator. Place the dough between two pieces of waxed paper and roll to ⅛ in/3 mm thick. Using cookie cutters, cut out as many shapes as possible. The dough is oily, so the cutter shouldn't stick to the dough. Using a spatula, place the shapes on the prepared sheets, spacing them at least 1 in/2.5 cm apart.

Bake until the cookies are dark brown, about 15 minutes. Remove to wire racks to cool completely. Let the sheets cool completely and repeat with the remaining dough.

TO MAKE THE ROYAL ICING / In a large bowl, whisk the egg whites until foamy. Add the confectioners' sugar and the cream of tartar and whisk until smooth. The mixture should be thick, but not so thick that it is a paste. Add water, 1 tsp at a time, if it is too thick. Cover the icing with plastic wrap until needed.

Decorate the cookies and let sit for about 1 hour to allow the icing to set.

Store in an airtight container, with waxed paper between the layers, at room temperature for up to 7 days.

CHOCOLATE CHIP COOKIES

2 cups/280 g Jeanne's Gluten-Free All-Purpose Flour (page 17)

1 tsp baking soda

1 tsp kosher salt

1 cup/225 g unsalted butter, at room temperature

1 cup/215 g packed dark brown sugar

½ cup/100 g granulated sugar

2 extra-large eggs, at room temperature

2 tsp pure vanilla extract

About 4 cups/680 g semisweet or bittersweet chocolate chips

1 cup/120 g chopped pecans, toasted (optional)

4 DOZEN COOKIES Chocolate chip cookies are my favorite cookie to make on a regular basis. You just can't go wrong with them. I've tried many, many recipes, and I always come back to this one, which is adapted from a recipe by Ina Garten, also known as the Barefoot Contessa. Garten is one of my cooking and baking goddesses, and she hit the ball out of the park with her recipe. The key is that it is chock full of chocolate chips. Also, the large grains of the kosher salt bring out the flavor of the chocolate. The recipe can easily be halved.

Preheat the oven to 350°F/180°C/gas mark 4. Line two cookie sheets with parchment paper.

In a medium bowl, mix together the flour, baking soda, and salt.

In the bowl of a stand mixer fitted with the paddle attachment, beat the butter on medium-high speed until light and fluffy, about 2 minutes. Add the brown and granulated sugars and beat for 2 minutes. Add the eggs, one at a time, beating after each addition. Then beat for 1 minute longer. Add the vanilla and beat until combined. Add the flour mixture and beat until just combined. Add the chocolate chips and the nuts (if using), and beat until combined.

Drop the dough by teaspoons onto the prepared sheets, spacing them about 1 in/2.5 cm apart (I do 12 cookies per sheet). Bake until the cookies are flat and brown, about 16 minutes. Let cool slightly on the cookie sheets, then remove to wire racks to cool completely. Let the sheets cool completely and repeat with the remaining dough.

Store in an airtight container at room temperature for up to 1 week.

CHOCOLATE CHIP
MERINGUES

ABOUT 45 SMALL COOKIES OR 30 BIG COOKIES Meringue cookies, made from egg whites whipped with sugar, are elegant and lighter than air. Once the cookies are baked, the outsides stay crunchy, while the insides are a bit chewy. When I add toasted nuts to the meringue, my preference is for pecans. You can use the leftover yolks to make Thumbprint Cookies (page 58).

3 egg whites

¼ tsp cream of tartar

¾ tsp pure vanilla extract

1 cup/200 g granulated sugar

1 cup/170 g regular or mini chocolate chips

1 cup/120 g toasted chopped nuts of your choice (optional)

Preheat the oven to 300°F/150°C/gas mark 2. Line two cookie sheets with parchment paper.

In the bowl of a stand mixer fitted with the whisk attachment, beat the egg whites on medium-high speed until foamy. Add the cream of tartar and beat for a few seconds to combine. Add the vanilla and beat for a few more seconds to combine. Increase the speed to high and beat until soft peaks form, about 3 minutes. Reduce the speed to low and sprinkle in the sugar a little bit at a time. Increase the speed to high and beat until stiff peaks form, about 10 minutes. Gently fold in the chocolate chips with a large spoon or rubber spatula. Fold in the nuts (if using).

Drop the meringue by heaping teaspoons or tablespoons (depending on how big you want them) onto the prepared sheets, spacing the cookies about 1½ in/4 cm apart. Bake for about 20 minutes for slightly chewy cookies or about 25 minutes for more crispy cookies. Carefully remove to wire racks to cool completely—the cookies will fall apart if you try to eat them too soon.

Store in an airtight container at room temperature for up to 5 days.

MERINGUE
MUSHROOMS

Meringue mushrooms are fun to make and to eat. I like to use some for the Bûche de Noël (page 75) and save the rest as stand-alone treats. These little gems are charming—they really look like mushrooms! The meringue is light and crunchy, offset by the rich chocolate, which adds a bit of elegance. The cookies do take a bit of work, but you will be rewarded by astonished *ooohs* and *ahhhs* from those lucky enough to get some. They are somewhat addictive because they are so small—you can't eat just one without wanting another (and another, and another).

2 egg whites

⅛ tsp cream of tartar

Pinch of salt

¼ tsp pure vanilla extract

½ cup/100 g granulated sugar

½ cup/80 g semisweet chocolate chips

1 Tbsp unsweetened cocoa powder

In the bowl of a stand mixer fitted with the whisk attachment, beat the egg whites on high speed until foamy, about 2 minutes. Add the cream of tartar, salt, and vanilla and continue to beat until the egg whites hold soft peaks, about 3 minutes. Reduce the speed to low and gradually sprinkle in the sugar so that it does not sink to the bottom. Increase the speed to high and whip until the mixture forms stiff, shiny peaks, about 10 minutes.

Preheat the oven to 225°F/110°C/gas ¼. Position a rack in the upper third of the oven and another rack in the lower third. Line two cookie sheets with parchment paper.

Fit a pastry bag with a medium-round tip (I use a #10 tip) and place the bag in a sturdy drinking glass to stabilize it while you fill it. Fill the bag halfway with the meringue. Twist the top and gently press down on the meringue to expel any air bubbles.

You are now going to pipe mushroom caps and stems. Be sure to pipe equal quantities of each. To pipe the caps, using a spiral motion,

squeeze out round mounds of meringue in a row down a prepared sheet. Pull the bag off each mound in a swirling motion to give the caps a spiral top. Try to pull the bag to the side to avoid forming peaks on the tops of the caps. You can make the caps as big as you'd like, although I don't recommend going any bigger than 2 in/5 cm in diameter. I like to pipe caps about 1 in/2.5 cm in diameter. For each row of caps, make a corresponding row of stems on the sheet. The meringue won't spread, so you don't need to give the caps and stems much room between them—about ½ in/12 mm is fine.

The stems can be a bit tricky. The easiest way to pipe them is to hold the bag and the tip vertically above the cookie sheet. Press out a spot of meringue, then with a subtle up-and-down motion, pull the bag straight up about 1 in/2.5 cm. This will give you a stem that looks like a tall, skinny elf cap. Or, you can make stems that have a wider base, making the elf cap a bit fatter. With either option, be sure that the tops of the stems have a point. This will make them easy to assemble with the caps later. Repeat piping rows of caps and stems until you use all the meringue. Wet the tip of a finger in water and carefully push down any peaks on the tops of the mushroom caps. This will make them easier to work with later.

Place the cookie sheets on the oven racks and bake until the meringue is dry, about 1 hour. The caps and stems should be crisp and dry enough to remove easily from the sheets. Let cool completely on the sheets on wire racks. This will take only a few minutes.

Next, you need to excavate a small hole in the middle of the underside of each cap to provide a place to attach the stem. With the tip of a toothpick, hollow out a small hole about ¼ in/6 mm in diameter and about ⅛ in/3 mm to ¼ in/ 6 mm in depth. Do this over a small plate so you can shake out the meringue dust.

In a small saucepan set over very low heat, melt the chocolate chips. Watch very carefully so the chocolate doesn't burn. Remove from the heat and whisk until smooth.

With the back of a teaspoon, spread a small amount of chocolate over the underside of each mushroom cap in a ring around the hole you just created. This mimics the dark gills on mushrooms. Work quickly—you want the chocolate to be just barely dry by the time you're ready to assemble the caps and the stems. Dip the tip, or pointy end, of a stem in the chocolate and then place it into the hole in the cap. Set the mushroom, cap-side down, on a lined sheet to set up. If your climate or kitchen is hot and humid, the chocolate will take longer to set. Don't worry if your stems are kind of wonky— that will add to the quirkiness of the mushrooms. If you end up with some caps that don't have stems, that's okay, too. They will look like tree fungi and, if used as decoration, are especially cute on the Bûche de Noël.

Place the cocoa powder in a small, shallow bowl. Lightly dip the top of each mushroom cap in the cocoa and lightly shake or brush off the extra cocoa. This mimics dirt on top of the mushrooms. After dipping every few mushrooms, fluff up the cocoa in the bowl with a spoon. The cocoa powder becomes flattened after several mushrooms are dipped.

Store in an airtight container at room temperature for up to 1 week. The container must be airtight; otherwise the mushrooms will absorb moisture from the air and become soft and squishy—more like marshmallows.

CHOCOLATE-CHERRY
BISCOTTI

ABOUT 4 DOZEN COOKIES As you may know, *biscotti* means "twice baked" in Italian. Biscotti are an Italian version of hard biscuits found around the world. They were originally created to feed travelers and soldiers, because their lack of moisture allowed them to be stored for long periods of time. Versions of these cookies abound in other cultures—they are known in the United States as hard tack, in Germany as *zwieback*, and in Jewish baking as *madelbrot*. Biscotti are excellent cookies for dunking—baking them twice ensures that they retain their shape and crunch when dipped into a hot beverage. My husband and I are tea drinkers, so we dunk them in our tea. My daughter is a hot cocoa drinker, so she dunks them in her cocoa (hey, you can never have too much chocolate, right?). Because of the cookies' terrific storage qualities (and delicious flavor), I like to have a tin of these ready for spur-of-the-moment visitors during the holiday season. For double-chocolate biscotti, substitute 1 cup/170 g regular or mini chocolate chips for the dried fruit.

2 cups/280 g Jeanne's Gluten-Free All-Purpose Flour (page 17)

½ cup/45 g unsweetened cocoa powder, sifted

¾ tsp baking soda

½ tsp baking powder

½ tsp salt

6 Tbsp/85 g unsalted butter, at room temperature

1 cup/200 g granulated sugar

2 extra-large eggs, at room temperature

1 cup/160 g chopped dried cherries or cranberries

Preheat the oven to 350°F/180°C/gas mark 4.

Line two cookie sheets with parchment paper.

In a medium bowl, mix together the flour, cocoa, baking soda, baking powder, and salt.

In a large bowl, using a large spoon, mix together the butter and sugar until well combined. Add the eggs, one at a time, stirring well after each addition. Stir in the flour mixture until just combined. Fold in the dried cherries. The dough will be very stiff.

Divide the dough in half and put the portions on opposite ends of one prepared cookie sheet. Shape each portion into a rough rectangle about 12 in/30.5 cm long by 4 in/10 cm wide by ½ in/12 mm thick. If you use your palms to shape the dough, it shouldn't stick to your hands, but if the dough does stick, wet your hands before continuing. You will now have two dough rectangles on your cookie sheet.

Bake the rectangles for 25 minutes. Let cool on the sheet for 20 minutes. Using a serrated knife, cut each rectangle on the cookie sheet crosswise, as you would a loaf of bread, into slices about ½ in/12 mm thick, cutting slowly and carefully so the slices don't crumble. Stand the slices upright on their bottoms on the two cookie sheets, spacing them ½ in/12 mm apart. The cookies should now look like the familiar biscotti.

Bake until the cookies are crisp and a finger pressed lightly on a cookie does not leave an imprint, about 15 minutes. Remove the cookies to wire racks to cool completely.

Store in an airtight container at room temperature for up to 1 week.

LEMON BARS

6 Tbsp/85 g unsalted butter, at room temperature, plus more for greasing

Tapioca flour for dusting

1 cup/200 g granulated sugar

1 cup/140 g Jeanne's Gluten-Free All-Purpose Flour (page 17), plus 2 Tbsp

2 extra-large eggs, at room temperature

1 Tbsp grated lemon zest

3 Tbsp freshly squeezed lemon juice

½ tsp baking powder

Confectioners' sugar for dusting

 16 BARS These bars make a lovely treat during the winter holidays. They add a bit of sassy sunshine to days of dreary weather. The bright color and tang are enough to perk up the coldest winter night. And they take advantage of the citrus that is in season at this time.

Preheat the oven to 350°F/180°C/gas mark 4. Grease an 8-by-8-in/20-by-20-cm baking pan with butter and dust with tapioca flour.

In a large bowl, using a hand mixer on medium speed, beat the butter until light and fluffy, about 2 minutes. Add ¼ cup/50 g of the granulated sugar and beat for about 1 minute. Beat in the 1 cup/140 g flour until combined. The mixture will look like wet sand with pebbles.

Press the mixture into the prepared pan. Bake until light brown, 18 to 20 minutes.

Meanwhile, place the eggs in a large bowl. Using the mixer on medium-high speed, beat until fluffy, about 3 minutes. Add the remaining ¾ cup/150 g granulated sugar and beat for

1 minute. Add the lemon zest and lemon juice and beat until combined. Add the 2 Tbsp flour and the baking powder and beat until combined.

Remove the pan from the oven. Pour the lemon mixture over the hot crust layer. Bake until the top is lightly browned around the edges and the center is set, about 15 minutes. Let cool in the pan on a wire rack. Sift confectioners' sugar in an even layer over top. Cut into sixteen 2-in/5-cm squares.

Store in an airtight container in the refrigerator for up to 5 days.

GINGERBREAD HOUSE

1 HOUSE PLUS DECORATIVE COOKIES

Gingerbread houses are a showstopping holiday treat. My grandmother made one each Christmas and sent it to us through the mail. It wasn't until I became an adult that I understood what a feat of engineering this was. And to be honest, I never made a good, solid gingerbread house until I wrote this book. After much experimenting, I found that the key to constructing a house out of cookie pieces is to take your time, use lots of thick royal icing for mortar, and have lots of canned goods to serve as structural supports. You will need to bake and assemble the house over the course of several hours or a couple of days.

Rather than make your own royal icing, you can use purchased royal icing powder (also called meringue powder) in a ratio of ½ cup/60 g powder to 2 tsp water. You want icing that is thick rather than runny. Add more icing powder if your mixture is too loose, or add more water if it is too thick.

For decorating the house, the sky's the limit. Go online to see what other people have done to their houses. Note that you want to use edible, gluten-free candies, cookies, and other decorations.

Dough for Gingerbread Cookies (page 59)

Royal Icing for Gingerbread Cookies (page 59)

Candies, cookies, and other decorations

Prepare the dough as directed and refrigerate for at least 1 hour, or up to 5 days.

You are going to roll out the dough directly onto parchment paper, cut out dough shapes, and then cut the parchment paper around the shapes in order to transport them to the baking sheets. The dough is too breakable and soft to transport large pieces with a spatula. Use the templates on pages 70–71 to cut out the following shapes from cardboard: 2 roof pieces, 2 side pieces, and 2 front/back pieces. Use cookie cutters of your choice to cut out trees, people, and other shapes for decorating.

Remove one piece of dough from the refrigerator. Place the dough on a large piece of parchment paper, top with a piece of waxed paper, and roll out to ¼ in/6 mm thick (no thinner). Using the templates and a sharp paring knife, cut out as many pieces as possible. Slowly and carefully remove each template. Do not remove the windows and door from inside the cutout pieces—they need to remain in place to make sure the pieces bake evenly. Carefully remove the dough scraps from around the pieces. Then, cut out the parchment paper around the pieces and carefully transfer them, each still on parchment, to a cookie sheet. The pieces will puff up and out a bit in the oven, so leave at least 1 in/2 cm between the pieces. Repeat the process with

CONTINUED /

the remaining dough. Roll out the scraps, cut out any shapes for decorating, and place on the cookie sheets.

Bake until the gingerbread pieces are light brown, 13 to 15 minutes. While the pieces are still hot, use the paring knife to cut around the windows and door, but don't remove these pieces until the gingerbread is completely cool. Let all the pieces cool on the cookie sheets.

To assemble the house, you will need a clean piece of cardboard that is bigger than the footprint of the house (about 8 by 10 in/20 by 25 cm). Use unopened food cans to help support the walls as you glue them together with the icing. You'll need at least seven cans. Have everything ready, and set up your work area in a place where you can let the house sit as it's being constructed. You will work on it, then leave it to set several times.

Before you start, tidy up and finish cutting the pieces, being sure to work slowly and carefully. With the paring knife, cut out the windows and the door (save the door piece.) With a serrated knife, straighten the sides of the house pieces, then use a Microplane grater to even them. Set the pieces next to each other to make sure they will fit fairly smoothly. Do any last-minute evening with the Microplane. Finally, stand each piece on the cardboard to make sure the bottom is fairly level. Time spent on this preparation will make the house assembly much easier.

Place a large dollop of icing in a pastry bag fitted with the plain tip. Have a sturdy glass handy for holding the pastry bag when it is not being used. Pipe a thick line of icing along the vertical edge of one side piece. Place on the cardboard base

and prop up between two cans. Place the edge of the one front piece against the side piece, so the edge of the side piece with the icing is now touching the side of the front piece. Prop up the front piece with two cans. Pipe icing along a vertical back edge of the other side piece and place against the other back edge of the front piece. Prop up the piece with two cans. Finally, pipe icing along the edges of the two side pieces and place the back piece against them. Place a can on the outside of this back piece.

Look at all the joined edges and straighten up any obviously crooked ones. The pieces aren't going to fit together perfectly. Pipe icing into any crevices. Then pipe a line of icing along the outside and inside edges of the entire footprint of the house, where the pieces meet the cardboard. This will help stabilize everything. The icing may drip down the sides of the house. That's okay—it will look like snow. Or, you can wipe it off as it drips. The thicker the icing, the less dripping you will have.

Let dry for at least 2 hours. Place the pastry bag in a lock-top bag to keep the icing it contains from drying out.

Before attaching the roof, remove the cans and make sure the walls are sturdy by trying to wiggle them gently. They should be solidly in place. Hold the roof pieces where they will go on the house. Note the distance between the bottom edges of the roof and the cardboard base. You will need something that matches this distance and can be used to support the roof pieces while they are drying. I use a coffee mug to support the bottom of each roof piece and place a can on top of the mug to prevent the piece from sliding outward. Pipe a thick line of icing along the slanted edge of one side of the front piece and the slanted edge of the same side of the back piece. Set a roof piece on the icing and add the chosen support. Repeat on the other side of the house with the remaining roof piece. Pipe more icing along all the crevices to add more support. The roof pieces may not fit together perfectly. You can pipe more icing along the crevices. It will look like snow. Later, you can use icing to attach candies along the top crevices.

Once the roof pieces are in place and well supported, let the house sit for at least 2 hours.

After the roof has set, decorate the house. Using the icing, you can draw designs like roof shingles and make little icicles that hang from the eaves. Be aware that the roof can collapse if too much weight is added. I usually pipe on shingles and icicles and put a line of icing or small candies along the top. You can attach cookie shutters to the windows, wafer shingles to the walls, and a candy wreath on the door (prop the reserved door piece so it looks ajar). You can add landscaping such as icing and candy paths and shrubs. If you baked cutout shapes such as trees and people, fix them upright with icing.

The house makes a spectacular centerpiece for the dining table. It should be quite sturdy and will last for at least 2 to 3 weeks.

All templates shown at 50 percent size,
please photocopy at 200 percent.

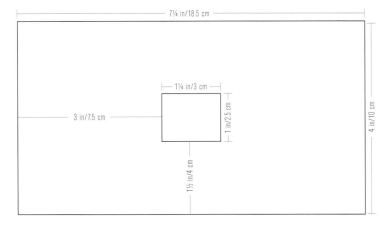

SIDES (MAKE 2)
4 in/10 cm by 7¼ in/18.5 cm

Window: 1¼ in/3 cm by 1 in/2.5 cm positioned 3 in/7.5 cm from
each side and 1½ in/4 cm from top to bottom

ROOF (MAKE 2)
4½ in/11.5 cm by 9 in/23 cm

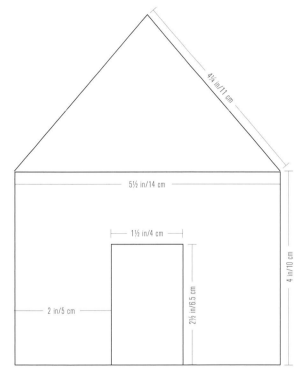

FRONT (MAKE ONE)

5½ in/14 cm wide by 4 in/10 cm tall, then angle to a point for another 4¼ in/11 cm

Door: Cut a doorway in the middle bottom 1½ in/4 cm wide by 2½ in/6.5 cm tall, positioned 2 in/5 cm from each side

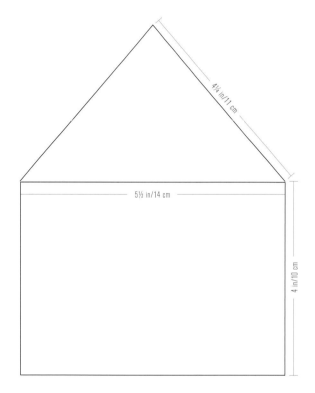

BACK (MAKE ONE)

5½ in/14 cm wide by 4 in/10 cm tall, then angle to a point for another 4¼ in/11 cm

03 CAKES

CAKES, TO ME, MEAN GATHERING WITH FRIENDS AND FAMILY. They can be made for casual eating or dressed up and served for the most fancy of occasions. If you think about it, cake is the most common choice for ceremonial and special events. Gluten-free flour is great for cakes because it has many of the qualities of the grade of wheat flour called cake flour, which is light and fluffy. I am often asked to bake cakes for my wheat-eating friends' special occasions. They think my cakes taste better and are lighter than the wheat counterparts.

In this chapter, I include cakes that I make for casual snacking, such as Cranberry Cake, Chocolate-Mandarin Cake, and Pound Cake. Other cakes are designed for or are traditional to winter are: Orange-Scented Olive Oil Cake (especially for Hanukkah), Bûche de Noël, fruitcake, and King Cake (traditional to Epiphany).

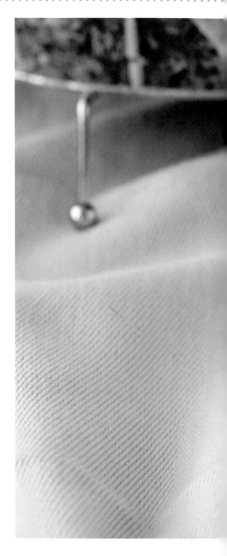

GENOISE

ONE 18-BY-13-IN/46-BY-33-CM CAKE This Italian sponge cake named after the town of Genoa is the basis of many French and Italian desserts. The recipe here is designed for the Bûche de Noël (facing page). You can also use it instead of the Pound Cake (page 89) for the Trifle (page 91). Genoise is special in that it is leavened entirely by eggs—without added leavener like baking powder or baking soda. The eggs are heated while being whisked with sugar in order to take advantage of the heat to help them rise. Once you understand the principles behind the cake, the batter is quite easy to make, and it's fun to watch the mixture triple in size. You may also eat this cake on its own, garnished with fresh fruit or jam and unsweetened whipped cream.

1 cup/140 g Jeanne's Gluten-Free All-Purpose Flour (page 17)

¼ tsp salt

6 extra-large eggs, at room temperature

1 cup/200 g granulated sugar

1 tsp pure vanilla extract

6 Tbsp/85 g unsalted butter, melted and cooled slightly

Preheat the oven to 350°F/180°C/gas mark 4. Line a half sheet pan with parchment paper.

In a small bowl, mix together the flour and salt. Sift the mixture three times.

Place the eggs and sugar in the bowl of a stand mixer. Choose a saucepan large enough to hold the bowl above the bottom of the pan. Fill the pan with 2 in/5 cm of water and bring to a gentle simmer. Place the bowl on the pan over (but not touching) the simmering water, and constantly whisk the egg mixture until the lower part of the bowl feels hot to the touch. This will only take a couple of minutes. Carefully remove the bowl from the pan. (You don't want to keep it over the simmering water for too long, or the eggs will scramble.) Place the bowl in the mixer and fit with the whisk attachment. Beat the egg mixture on high speed until it triples in volume, about 7 minutes. Add the vanilla and beat just to combine.

Remove the bowl from the mixer. Lightly sprinkle the flour mixture over the egg mixture in three batches, and carefully fold each batch into the egg mixture with a rubber spatula. Be sure to scrape the bottom of the bowl—the flour tends to settle. Gently and slowly pour the melted butter into the side of the mixture— don't pour it directly in the middle, as that will deflate the volume you've created. Gently fold in the butter, making sure it is thoroughly combined. This will take a bit of folding, so keep going and be patient. Pour the batter into the prepared pan, making sure it is evenly distributed. Gently smooth the top.

Bake until the cake is light brown on the top, about 15 minutes. Let the cake cool in the pan on a wire rack. If not using immediately, carefully wrap the cooled cake, in the pan, in aluminum foil and store at room temperature for up to 2 days.

BÛCHE DE NOËL

ABOUT 14 SERVINGS This fun cake, whose French name translates as "Christmas log," represents the special Yule log that is burned on the hearth as part of Christmas celebrations. The rich egg cake is frosted with coffee buttercream, rolled into a log shape, and then covered with chocolate buttercream. Although the cake looks difficult to make, it's quite easy—it just requires time and patience. The ideas for decorating are endless. This version gives two options: using confectioners' sugar as snow and adorning with Meringue Mushrooms.

1 cup/200 g granulated sugar

3 egg whites, at room temperature

¼ tsp salt

1½ cup/340 g unsalted butter, at room temperature, plus 1 Tbsp

1 tsp vanilla extract

⅓ cup/75 ml warm, strong coffee or espresso (decaffeinated, if desired)

3½ oz/100 g semisweet chocolate

Genoise (facing page)

Confectioners' sugar for dusting (optional)

Meringue Mushrooms (page 62; optional)

Place the granulated sugar, egg whites, and salt in the bowl of a stand mixer. Choose a saucepan large enough to hold the bowl above the bottom of the pan. Fill the pan with 2 in/5 cm of water and bring to a gentle simmer. Place the bowl on the pan over (but not touching) the simmering water, and constantly whisk the egg mixture until the sugar is dissolved and the bottom of the bowl feels hot to the touch. This will only take a few minutes. Carefully remove the bowl from the pan. (Don't keep the bowl over the simmering water for too long, or the eggs will scramble.)

Place the bowl in the mixer and fit with the whisk attachment. Beat the egg mixture on medium-high speed until it triples in volume, about 6 minutes. Reduce the speed to medium and add the 1½ cups/340 g butter, 1 Tbsp at a time. Increase the speed to medium-high and beat until the mixture is smooth and there are no lumps. The buttercream will probably go through a stage where it looks curdled—that's normal. Just keep mixing until it smooths out again. This will take several minutes. Add the

vanilla and beat until combined. Divide the buttercream in half, leaving one half in the mixer bowl and placing the second half in another bowl.

Add the coffee to the buttercream in the mixer and beat on medium-high speed with the whisk attachment until smooth. (The coffee must be added warm, but not hot, so it will mix with the buttercream. If it's too cold, you will need to place the bowl back on the pan over the simmering water and whisk until the mixture has warmed up enough to combine. This shouldn't take too long, and you don't want to warm the mixture too much. Once it starts to combine, return the bowl to the mixer and beat the buttercream on medium-high until combined.)

In a small pan over very low heat, melt the chocolate and the remaining 1 Tbsp butter. Watch carefully so the mixture doesn't burn. Remove from the heat and whisk until smooth. Add the chocolate mixture—it should be warm but not hot—to the remaining buttercream. Place the bowl in the mixer and beat on medium

CONTINUED /

speed with the whisk attachment until combined. (I find that the chocolate is somewhat hard to mix in completely. What I do is remove the bowl from the mixer as soon as the mixture looks combined and then stir by hand to make sure all the chocolate is completely incorporated. Don't worry if you see a few streaks here and there—they will add to the charm of the cake because the frosting will be decorated to look like tree bark.)

Frost the top of the genoise with the coffee buttercream, using the whole batch (this will end up being the inside of the cake). Now, you will roll the cake. It's not hard, but you need to go slowly. Using a spatula, lift up the cake, including the parchment paper, from one of the narrow sides. Gradually and firmly start to roll the cake, using the parchment paper to push the cake and removing the parchment as you roll (don't roll the parchment into the cake). Roll the cake as tightly as you can while being gentle and firm. Place the rolled cake on a serving platter, seam-side down.

If you would like to create a "branch" for the bûche de nöel, use a ruler to measure 2 in/5 cm from one end of the rolled cake. With a sharp knife, make a slanted cut from the corner of the end to the 2-in/5-cm mark. This end of the cake is now angled. Arrange this cut-off wedge so that the slanted side is against the side of the cake and the wedge rests on the platter. Using the chocolate buttercream, "glue" the wedge to the cake.

Frost the entire outside of the cake, including the ends, with the chocolate buttercream. If you like, run the tines of a fork lengthwise through the buttercream, wiggling and swirling the fork a bit, to simulate the grooves in tree bark. Do the same on the branch if you have one. Using a toothpick, draw a spiral in the buttercream on the ends of the cake and on the end of the cut branch to imitate tree rings.

If desired, sift confectioners' sugar over the top to simulate snow and decorate with the meringue mushrooms.

This cake is best the day you make it. It may be stored, lightly wrapped in plastic wrap (especially the cut ends), at room temperature for 1 day or in the refrigerator for up to 3 days. The buttercream will become hard when cold, so bring the cake to room temperature before serving.

FRUITCAKE

10 TO 15 SERVINGS

For me, fruitcake evokes the picture-perfect Christmas, with snow, caroling, a fire in the hearth, and thoughts of Santa. And a good fruitcake means a dense cake filled with both candied and dried fruits. The inspiration for this recipe came from a fruitcake by Laurie Colwin, one of my favorite food writers, who in turn found her inspiration from Jane Grigson, an English food writer. The trick to making the perfect fruitcake is to macerate, or soak, the dried fruits in liquor at least overnight. This way, the fruits are full of liquid and don't suck out the moisture from the cake, which is what causes some fruitcakes to be too dry. My father-in-law, a self-proclaimed fruitcake expert, has deemed this the perfect fruitcake. Don't let the recipe fool you—it looks complicated, but the only complicated part is gathering all the fruits. You can use the combination here or experiment with your own mixture—just be sure the total weight is the same.

When the time comes to "decant" the cake (take it out of the wrapping), the traditional finish is to glaze it with slightly warmed jelly or jam. Or, you can serve the cake as is. Leftover slices may be toasted and eaten with butter and jam for breakfast.

MACERATED FRUIT

2½ lb/1.2 kg raisins, pitted prunes, pitted dates, and dried figs, finely chopped

½ cup/60 g candied orange and/or lemon peel, finely chopped

⅓ cup/60 g candied or dried cherries, finely chopped

⅔ cup/85 g candied or preserved ginger, finely chopped

Grated zest and juice of 1 large lemon

Grated zest and juice of 1 large orange

1 Tbsp orange or tangerine marmalade

1 Tbsp apricot jam

1 cup/240 ml applesauce

2 Tbsp brandy, sweet sherry, or apple juice

1 cup/225 g unsalted butter, at room temperature, plus more for greasing

3 cups/420 g Jeanne's Gluten-Free All-Purpose Flour (page 17)

1 tsp ground cinnamon

1 tsp ground ginger

CONTINUED /

THE DAY BEFORE YOU BAKE THE CAKE, PREPARE THE MACERATED FRUIT / Place the raisins, prunes, dates, and figs in a large bowl. Add the citrus peel, cherries, ginger, lemon zest and juice, and orange zest and juice. Add the marmalade, jam, applesauce, and brandy and stir to combine. Cover the bowl and let stand overnight at room temperature so that the fruits soak up the liquid and the flavors meld. The mixture can macerate in the refrigerator for up to 1 week.

Preheat the oven to 325°F/165°C/gas mark 3. If the fruit has been in the refrigerator, bring it to room temperature. Grease the bottom and sides of 9½- or 10-in/24- or 25-cm springform pan with butter. Line the bottom with three layers of parchment paper and the sides with one layer of parchment. The batter will be very sticky.

In a medium bowl, mix together the flour, cinnamon, ginger, nutmeg, allspice, and baking powder.

In the bowl of a stand mixer fitted with the paddle attachment, beat the butter on medium-high speed until light and fluffy, about 3 minutes. Add the brown sugar and beat for 1 minute. Reduce the speed to low, add the vanilla, and beat until combined. Add the eggs, one at a time, beating after each addition. Then beat for 1 minute longer. Add the flour mixture and beat until just combined. Add the macerated fruit and, with a large

CONTINUED /

1 tsp freshly grated nutmeg

1 tsp ground allspice

1 Tbsp baking powder

1 cup/215 g packed
dark brown sugar

1 tsp pure vanilla extract

4 extra-large eggs, at room
temperature

2 Tbsp brandy, rum, whisky,
sweet sherry, or apple juice,
or as needed

wooden spoon, combine with the batter. This requires a bit of strength—you can count it as your exercise for the day. Scrape the batter into the prepared pan.

Bake for 2 hours, then reduce the oven temperature to 300°F/150°C/gas mark 2 and bake until a toothpick inserted into the middle of the cake comes out clean, about 2 hours. If the cake browns too quickly, you might want to tent it with aluminum foil for the last 2 hours so it doesn't burn.

Remove the cake from oven and, while it is still hot, pierce it all over with a skewer. Pour the brandy over the top. Place the pan on a wire rack and let the cake cool completely.

Remove the sides from the pan and peel the parchment paper from the sides and bottom of the cake. Wrap the cake in waxed paper and place it in an airtight container or wrap in a few layers of plastic wrap. Leave the cake at room temperature for 3 to 5 days to allow the flavors to meld. If you used alcohol, you may store the cake in the refrigerator for up to 2 weeks.

Once the cake is sliced, store in an airtight container at room temperature for up to 1 week.

CRANBERRY CAKE

10 TO 15 SERVINGS This basic butter cake is perfect for using cranberries in more than just a Thanksgiving side dish. I prefer fresh cranberries if I can find them, but frozen ones are fine, too. Add them to the batter in a semifrozen state—this will help them retain their shape during baking. What makes this simple cake stand out is the little pops of tart cranberry tucked into the rich cake. I usually serve the cake as is, but you can dust it with confectioners' sugar or garnish each serving with a dollop of whipped cream.

Preheat the oven to 350°F/180°C/gas mark 4. Line the bottom of a 9½- or 10-in/24- or 25-cm springform pan with parchment paper. Grease the sides of the pan with butter and dust with tapioca flour.

In a small bowl, mix together the 1 cup/140 g all-purpose flour, baking powder, and salt.

In a large bowl, using a hand mixer on medium-high speed, beat the butter and sugar until light and fluffy, about 2 minutes. Add the vanilla and beat to combine. Add the eggs, one at a time, beating after each addition. Reduce the speed to medium and beat for 1 minute. Add the flour mixture and beat until just combined. Carefully spoon the batter into the prepared pan. This is a thick batter, so you will need to stabilize the parchment paper with a finger so it doesn't shift to one side.

In a medium bowl, combine the cranberries and the 1½ tsp flour. Spoon the cranberries evenly over the batter.

Bake until a toothpick inserted into the middle of the cake comes out clean, 60 to 70 minutes. Let the cake cool in the pan for about 10 minutes. Run a knife around the sides to release the cake from the pan, then remove the outer ring and set the cake on a wire rack to cool.

Store, tightly wrapped, at room temperature for up to 5 days.

½ cup/115 g unsalted butter, at room temperature, plus more for greasing

Tapioca flour for dusting

1 cup/140 g Jeanne's Gluten-Free All-Purpose Flour (page 17), plus 1½ tsp

1 tsp baking powder

½ tsp kosher salt

1 cup/200 g granulated sugar

½ tsp pure vanilla extract

2 extra-large eggs, at room temperature

2 cups/225 g fresh cranberries or frozen cranberries, slightly thawed

GINGERBREAD CAKE WITH PERSIMMON

½ cup/115 g unsalted butter, plus more for greasing

Tapioca flour for dusting

2 cups/280 g Jeanne's Gluten-Free All-Purpose Flour (page 17)

½ cup/80 g gluten-free cornmeal, preferably medium-grind

½ tsp salt

1 tsp ground cinnamon

½ tsp ground cloves

½ tsp ground ginger

½ tsp freshly grated nutmeg

2 tsp baking soda

2 tsp baking powder

½ cup/100 g granulated sugar

1 cup/240 ml unsulphured molasses

2 extra-large eggs, at room temperature

1 cup/240 ml boiling water

2 tsp peeled and grated fresh ginger

2 ripe but firm Fuyu persimmons, peeled and diced

16 SERVINGS My friend Jenifer, who is from Arkansas, loves to cook. She learned at the knee of her grandmother, whom she called Nanny. One day a few autumns ago, I heard about a fabulous gingerbread cake recipe that Nanny had given to Jenifer. I begged Jenifer to share the recipe with me, since I am a Southern girl at heart.

What makes this cake extra special is that it has a surprise ingredient: persimmons. These round, bright orange tree fruits look like large orange tomatoes and have an interior texture somewhat like that of a plum. The taste is subtle, a combination of plums and dates. Persimmon season is October through December, which means the fruits are ripe by Thanksgiving. This cake has a delicate crumb and a light gingerbread flavor. The spices are nicely offset by the subtle sweetness of the diced persimmons dotted throughout the cake. I've adapted the recipe to be gluten-free. Thank you, Jenifer and Nanny!

If you can't find persimmons or don't want to use them, you may make a plain gingerbread cake. With or without the persimmons, the cake is excellent garnished with whipped cream.

Preheat the oven to 350°F/180°C/gas mark 4. Grease an 8-in/20-cm square baking pan with butter and dust with tapioca flour.

In a medium bowl, mix together the all-purpose flour, cornmeal, salt, cinnamon, cloves, ground ginger, nutmeg, baking soda, and baking powder.

In the bowl of a stand mixer fitted with the paddle attachment, beat the butter on medium-high speed until light and fluffy, about 1 minute. Add the sugar and beat for 1 minute. Add the molasses and beat for 1 minute. Add the eggs, one at a time, beating after each addition. Then beat for 1 minute longer. Add the flour mixture and beat until just combined.

Reduce the speed to low and slowly pour the boiling water into the side of the batter so the water doesn't splash out of the bowl. Carefully beat, alternately stopping and starting, until just combined. Add the fresh ginger and persimmons and mix by hand with a spoon until just incorporated. Scrape into the prepared pan.

Bake until a toothpick inserted into the middle of the cake comes out clean, about 50 minutes. Let the cake cool in the pan for about 5 minutes, then unmold and place on a wire rack. Serve warm, cut into 2-in/5-cm squares, or let cool completely before serving.

Store, tightly wrapped, at room temperature for up to 3 days.

CHOCOLATE-MANDARIN CAKE

10 TO 15 SERVINGS One thing I like about December is that mandarin oranges are in season. When I lived in New York City, I remember stopping at the deli around the corner from my apartment to pick up a few clementines (a kind of mandarin) each day on my walk to the university. It was like having a bit of sunshine in my pocket on those cold and snowy days. Clementines are sometimes called the "Christmas orange" because they come into season near Christmas. Now that I live in Seattle, satsumas are the mandarin orange of choice in most grocery stores. This cake takes full advantage of mandarin season. I prefer to bake with fresh fruit whenever I can, and this is a perfect way to do so in winter. The cake is not too sweet because it uses whole satsumas, peels and all, which makes it ideal for afternoon tea. The original recipe came to me via my dear friend Kim, who was also gluten intolerant. Before you start mixing the batter, the oranges need to be cooked. This takes about an hour, filling your house with an alluring aroma.

4 small mandarin oranges such as clementines or satsumas

Melted unsalted butter for greasing

Tapioca flour for dusting

2 cups/280 g Jeanne's Gluten-Free All-Purpose Flour (page 17)

½ cup/45 g unsweetened cocoa powder, sifted

1 tsp baking powder

½ tsp baking soda

½ tsp salt

5 extra-large eggs

1 cup/200 g granulated sugar

1 cup/170 g semisweet chocolate chips (optional)

Confectioners' sugar for dusting (optional)

Whipped cream for serving (optional)

Scrub the oranges thoroughly. Do not peel them. Place the oranges in a medium saucepan and cover with water. Bring to a boil over high heat, cover, and reduce the heat to a gentle simmer. Cook until the oranges are soft, about 1 hour.

Set a wire rack on a cookie sheet. Drain the oranges and place on the rack to cool completely. If you want to cool them quickly, immerse them in a large bowl of ice water. Put the cooled oranges in a food processor and pulse until smooth.

Preheat the oven to 350°F/180°C/gas mark 4. Using a pastry brush, thoroughly grease a 9- to 10-cup/2.1- to 2.4-L Bundt pan with melted butter, making sure that all the nooks and crannies are covered. Dust with tapioca flour.

In a medium bowl, mix together the all-purpose flour, cocoa powder, baking powder, baking soda, and salt.

In the bowl of a stand mixer fitted with the whisk attachment, beat the eggs and granulated sugar on medium-high speed until light and fluffy, about 5 minutes. Reduce the speed to low, add the flour mixture, and beat until just combined. Add the puréed oranges and beat on low until just combined. Stir a few times with a spoon, scraping the bottom of the bowl to incorporate any unmixed flour into the batter. Stir in the chocolate chips (if using). Scrape the batter into the prepared pan.

Bake until a toothpick inserted into the middle of the cake comes out clean, about 1 hour. Let the cake cool in the pan for 10 minutes. Carefully unmold the cake onto a wire rack and let cool completely. Because the cake is not very sweet, it's nice dusted with confectioners' sugar. If you like, serve slices of the cake with whipped cream.

Store, loosely covered, at room temperature for up to 5 days.

ORANGE-SCENTED OLIVE OIL CAKE

10 TO 15 SERVINGS This recipe is particularly appropriate for Hanukkah, a holiday that celebrates, among other things, the miracle of oil. Once the Jews took back their holy temple, they found that there was only enough consecrated oil to last for one day—yet it actually lasted for eight days. This cake is light and has a fine, delicate crumb. A good-quality olive oil is important here because the taste definitely shines through.

Preheat the oven to 325°F/165°C/gas mark 3. Using a pastry brush, thoroughly grease a 9- to 10-cup/2.1- to 2.4-L Bundt pan with olive oil, making sure that all the nooks and crannies are covered. Dust with tapioca flour.

In a small bowl, mix together the all-purpose flour, salt, and baking powder.

In the bowl of a stand mixer fitted with the whisk attachment, beat the eggs and sugar on medium-high speed until the mixture is light and fluffy and tripled in size, about 10 minutes. Reduce the speed to low and slowly pour the olive oil into the side of the mixture—don't pour it directly in the middle, as that will deflate the volume you've created. Increase the speed to

high and beat for 2 minutes. Reduce the speed to low, add the orange zest, and beat until combined. Add the flour mixture and beat until just combined. (I recommend removing the bowl from the mixer and using a rubber spatula to scrape the bottom of the bowl to make sure all the flour is incorporated.) Scrape the batter into the prepared pan.

Bake until a toothpick inserted in the middle of the cake comes out clean, about 1 hour. Let the cake cool in the pan for 5 minutes, then unmold onto a wire rack and let cool completely.

Store, lightly covered, at room temperature for up to 5 days.

1¾ cups/420 ml good-quality extra-virgin olive oil, plus more for greasing

Tapioca flour for dusting

2 cups/280 g Jeanne's Gluten-Free All-Purpose Flour (page 17)

1 tsp salt

2 tsp baking powder

5 extra-large eggs, at room temperature

1¼ cups/250 g granulated sugar

1 Tbsp grated orange or tangerine zest

KING CAKE

½ cup/115 g unsalted butter, at room temperature, plus more for greasing

Tapioca flour for dusting

4 cups/560 g Jeanne's Gluten-Free All-Purpose Flour (page 17)

1 tsp freshly grated nutmeg

2 tsp salt

1 tsp grated lemon zest

1 Tbsp granulated sugar, plus ½ cup/100 g

¾ cup/180 ml warm water

2 Tbsp active dry yeast

1 extra-large egg, at room temperature; 4 egg yolks, at room temperature ; plus 1 extra-large egg mixed with 1 Tbsp milk, for egg wash

½ cup/120 ml warm milk (about 110°F/43°C)

½ tsp ground cinnamon

1 *fève* (see headnote) or 1 dried bean

ICING

3 cups/340 g confectioners' sugar, sifted

¼ cup/60 ml freshly squeezed lemon juice

10 TO 15 SERVINGS Named for the Three Wise Men, King Cake is traditionally eaten on Epiphany, or Twelfth Night, which falls on January 6. In the Christian tradition, Twelfth Night is the last day of the Twelve Days of Christmas, the day that the Three Wise Men arrived to see the baby Jesus. The cake contains a small (about 1 in/2.5 cm) porcelain (or plastic) trinket shaped like a baby, called a *fève*, to symbolize Jesus. Nowadays, *fèves* come in a variety of shapes in addition to babies, including popular cartoon characters. The person who gets the trinket has the honor of providing the cake for the next year's celebration (or, in some traditions, the whole party!). King Cake is basically a brioche, a yeasted cake. The yeast makes the dough rise higher than for a normal cake, the sugar allows the cake to maintain a fine crumb, and the egg yolks give it a richness fit for royalty. What this means is that the cake is lightly sweet and delicate on the tongue, with a hint of nutmeg and lemon to flirt with your tastebuds. The icing gives the cake a sweet-tangy finish that makes it irresistible.

Grease a 9-in/23-cm tube pan with butter and dust with tapioca flour.

In a medium bowl, mix together the all-purpose flour, nutmeg, salt, and lemon zest.

In a small bowl, whisk the 1 Tbsp granulated sugar into the warm water until dissolved. Whisk in the yeast until dissolved. Set aside to proof. The mixture will get foamy.

In the bowl of a stand mixer fitted with the paddle attachment, beat the butter and ½ cup/100 g granulated sugar on medium speed until fluffy, about 3 minutes. Reduce the speed to low and add the whole egg and the egg yolks, one at a time, beating after each addition. Increase the speed to medium and beat for about 2 minutes longer. Add the flour mixture alternately with the warm milk in small batches, beginning and ending with the flour mixture. Beat until just combined. Add the yeast mixture a bit at a time, beating after each addition until just combined. You'll need to add the yeast mixture gradually so it does not splash out of the bowl. The dough will be very thick. Increase the speed to medium-high and beat for 3 minutes.

Spoon the dough into the prepared pan and smooth the top. Sprinkle the cinnamon evenly over the top. Cover with plastic wrap and set aside to rise until doubled in bulk, about 1 hour. Preheat the oven to 375°F/190°C/gas mark 5. (I usually put the pan on top of my stove to take advantage of the warmth from the preheating oven.)

Remove the plastic wrap and gently brush the top of the cake with the egg wash. Bake until a toothpick inserted into the

CONTINUED /

middle of the cake comes out clean, 25 to 35 minutes. An instant-read thermometer inserted into the middle will read at least 190°F/88°C. If the top starts to brown too quickly, loosely tent the cake with aluminum foil toward the end of baking.

If your pan has removable sides, remove them and place the cake, still in the bottom of the pan, on a wire rack. Be very careful—this can be tricky with a tube pan. When the cake has cooled enough to handle it, remove it from the pan and let cool on the wire rack. If the cake does not have removable sides, very carefully turn out the cake onto the wire rack. Then turn it upright to cool. Press the *fève* into the cake at a random spot on the bottom.

TO MAKE THE ICING / In a large bowl, whisk together the confectioners' sugar and lemon juice. If the icing is too thick, add up to 3 Tbsp water, 1 Tbsp at a time, whisking until smooth. The consistency should be somewhere between thick enough to be spreadable and thin enough to be drizzled.

Spread or drizzle the icing on the cake, letting it drip over the sides. You can use a rubber spatula to move the icing around.

The cake is best eaten the day it is baked. If you need to store it, wrap tightly in plastic wrap and store at room temperature for up to 5 days. To refresh the texture, microwave or toast pieces of the cake.

POUND CAKE

10 TO 15 SERVINGS I have something of a love affair with pound cake. I can't get enough of it. On my blog, I have something like ten recipes for different types of pound cake. Of all of them, this is my favorite, a basic pound cake perfect for any occasion. It is simple and easy to make, and can be used as a stand-alone cake or in other recipes. This version is inspired by a recipe created by Edna Lewis, one of my favorite Southern U.S. chefs and food writers. The cake is excellent on its own or spread with jam, or with a dollop of unsweetened whipped cream on the side. It also serves as the base for Trifle (page 91).

1 cup/225 g unsalted butter, at room temperature, plus more for greasing

Tapioca flour for dusting

2¼ cups/315 g Jeanne's Gluten-Free All-Purpose Flour (page 17)

¼ tsp salt

1⅔ cups/330 g granulated sugar

1 Tbsp pure vanilla extract

1 tsp freshly squeezed lemon juice

4 extra-large eggs, at room temperature

Preheat the oven to 350°F/180°C/gas mark 4. Grease a 9-in/23-cm tube pan with butter and dust with tapioca flour.

In a medium bowl, mix together the all-purpose flour and salt.

In the bowl of a stand mixer fitted with the paddle attachment, beat the butter and sugar on medium-high speed until white and very fluffy, about 5 minutes. Reduce the speed to medium, add the vanilla and lemon juice, and beat until combined. Add the eggs, one at a time, beating after each addition. Then beat for 2 minutes longer. Reduce the speed to low, add the flour mixture, and beat until just combined.

Scrape the batter into the prepared pan and smooth the top. Thump the pan on the counter once to release any trapped air bubbles. Bake until a toothpick inserted into the middle comes out clean, about 1 hour. Let the cake cool in the pan on a wire rack for 5 minutes. Run a spatula or butter knife around the edge of the cake to release it from the pan and then carefully (especially if your tube pan is in two pieces) turn out onto the rack. Turn the cake upright and let cool completely.

Store, tightly covered, at room temperature for up to 5 days.

TRIFLE

One of my all-time favorite English desserts, trifle is basically a layered confection that includes cake, alcohol, jam, pastry cream, and fruit, topped with whipped cream. It is a show-stopping dessert. This recipe uses either of two cakes in this chapter and allows you to choose your favorite jam and fruits. You can substitute orange or apple juice for the liqueur. During the holiday season, I like to use a combination of frozen berries and frozen peaches, or sliced bananas and orange segments. Trifle is not hard to make, but it takes a bit of time to make the cake and the pastry cream and to assemble the dessert. I recommend that you read through the directions before starting.

Pound Cake (page 89) or Genoise (page 74), cut into 36 roughly equal slices

6 Tbsp/90 ml Grand Marnier, brandy, sweet sherry, or liqueur of your choice

¾ cup/180 ml jam of your choice

6 cups/750 g sliced fruits of your choice plus more for garnish (optional)

Pastry Cream (page 92)

1½ cups/360 ml chilled heavy cream

Have all the ingredients ready. For the first layer, arrange 12 cake pieces like fallen dominoes around the bottom of a trifle bowl or another glass bowl about 8½ in/21.5 cm in diameter and 5 in/12 cm deep. Sprinkle the cake layer evenly with 2 Tbsp of the liqueur. Spoon on ¼ cup/60 ml of the jam and smooth out so the pieces are equally covered. Arrange a third of the fruit on top of the jam so that the jam is somewhat equally covered. If the fruit is frozen, use it in its frozen state—this will allow the fruit to defrost and release more liquid onto the cake as it sets. Spread 1 cup/240 ml of the pastry cream on top of the fruit. Repeat the layers twice, to make a total of three layers.

Cover the bowl with plastic wrap and refrigerate for at least 24 hours or up to 3 days. The longer the trifle sits, the more the flavors meld and the cake becomes saturated with the moisture.

Just before serving, place the chilled cream in the bowl of a stand mixer fitted with the whisk attachment. Beat until the cream forms just barely stiff peaks. (Don't whip it too long because it will turn into butter.) Smooth the whipped cream over the chilled trifle and garnish with more fruit if desired. Serve by removing large spoonfuls from the bowl, being sure to get all the layers in each serving.

Store, tightly covered, in the refrigerator for up to 5 days.

PASTRY CREAM
3 CUPS/720 ML PASTRY CREAM

6 egg yolks, at room temperature
½ cup/100 g granulated sugar
½ cup/70 g Jeanne's Gluten-Free All-Purpose Flour (page 17)
Pinch of salt
2½ cups/600 ml milk
1 Tbsp pure vanilla extract

In a large, heatproof bowl, whisk the egg yolks and sugar. Sift in the flour and salt and whisk to combine. This will create a loose paste. Don't let the egg mixture sit too long, or the sugar will cook the eggs by a chemical reaction.

In a heavy-bottomed saucepan over medium heat, bring the milk to just simmering. Do not let it boil. Slowly add the hot milk to the egg mixture, whisking constantly to avoid cooking the eggs. (To keep the bowl from moving around, place it on a kitchen towel.) Whisk the mixture until smooth.

Pour the mixture into the saucepan and cook over medium heat until just boiling. Constantly move the whisk through the mixture, but don't actually whisk it—the bubbles created by whisking will confuse you about when the mixture starts to simmer. When the mixture reaches a simmer, whisk constantly until it thickens, 30 to 60 seconds. Remove from heat and whisk in the vanilla. Whisk until the pastry cream is smooth. If some of the egg cooked and you can see chunks in the pastry cream, strain it through a sieve.

Pour the pastry cream into a clean bowl and cover with a disk of waxed paper placed directly on the cream so that a film does not form on top. Let cool to room temperature and then refrigerate for up to 3 days. Whisk before using to remove any lumps.

TOASTED PECAN SNACK CAKE

16 SERVINGS Kwanzaa incorporates many Southern dishes in its dessert traditions. This cake, though nice anytime, is perfect to serve during Kwanzaa because pecans are native to the American South and are integral to Southern cooking. This cake gets rave reviews when I serve it to guests. The toasted pecans add crunch and a rich, savory undertone to the simple butter cake base, for a winning combination. As you've probably figured out, I adore pecans! Anytime I need to use nuts, pecans are the ones I turn to.

8 Tbsp/115 g unsalted butter, at room temperature

1⅓ cups/160 g chopped pecans

1½ cups/210 g Jeanne's Gluten-Free All-Purpose Flour (page 17)

1½ tsp baking powder

¼ tsp salt

¾ cup/150 g granulated sugar

1 tsp pure vanilla extract

2 extra-large eggs, at room temperature

½ cup/120 ml milk

Preheat the oven to 350°F/180°C/gas mark 4. Line the bottom of a 8-in/20-cm square baking pan with parchment paper.

In a small, heavy skillet, melt 1 Tbsp of the butter over medium heat. Add the pecans and cook, stirring often, until toasted, about 5 minutes. Watch carefully so that the nuts don't burn. Put aside to cool.

In a small bowl, mix together the flour, baking powder, and salt.

In a large bowl, using a hand mixer on medium-high speed, beat the remaining butter until light and fluffy, about 2 minutes. Add the sugar and beat for 1 minute. Add the vanilla and beat until combined. Add the eggs, one at a time, beating after each addition. Then beat for 1 minute more. Add the flour mixture and the milk alternately in little batches, beginning and ending with the flour mixture. Reduce the speed to medium and beat for a few seconds to be sure the mixture is completely combined. With a rubber spatula, fold in the pecans.

Scrape the batter into the prepared pan and smooth the top. Bake until a toothpick inserted into the middle of the cake comes out clean, 30 to 35 minutes. Let the cake cool in the pan for 5 minutes. Then unmold onto a wire rack, remove the parchment paper, turn the cake top up, and let cool completely. Cut into 2-in/5-cm squares to serve.

Store, tightly wrapped, at room temperature for up to 5 days.

STEAMED PLUM PUDDING

1 cup/225 g unsalted butter, melted and cooled to room temperature, plus more for greasing

Tapioca flour for dusting

3 cups/300 g lightly packed fresh gluten-free white bread crumbs, made from Soft Sandwich Bread (page 125)

1 cup/145 g raisins, preferably golden, coarsely chopped

1 cup/120 g dried currants, coarsely chopped

1 cup/160 g dried cherries or cranberries, coarsely chopped

1 tsp ground cinnamon

½ tsp freshly grated nutmeg

1⅓ cups/265 g granulated sugar

4 extra-large eggs, at room temperature, lightly beaten

½ tsp vanilla extract

½ cup/120 ml orange or tangerine marmalade

½ cup/120 ml rum, brandy, or apple juice

HARD SAUCE

1 cup/230 g unsalted butter at room temperature

¾ cup/ 160 g packed dark brown sugar

2 Tbsp rum, brandy or sherry, or 2 tsp pure vanilla extract

8 TO 10 SERVINGS As you may know, in England the word *pudding* connotes "dessert," so an English pudding isn't necessarily what Americans and others outside England think of as "pudding." Also there are no plums in traditional plum pudding. *Plum* is used to denote any kind of dried fruit. This recipe was inspired by one made by Julia Child, who is among my baking goddesses. It is traditionally served with a hard sauce, which is more of a buttery spread. Although plum pudding isn't widely known outside England, there is a reason why it's popular—it's amazingly good. This is one of my husband's all-time favorite desserts.

Using a pastry brush, grease a 2-qt/2-L pudding mold with melted butter, making sure that all the nooks and crannies are covered. Dust with tapioca flour.

Place the bread crumbs in a large bowl and add the raisins, currants, cherries, cinnamon, and nutmeg. Mix with a big spoon until combined. Add the granulated sugar and mix until combined. Add the butter and stir well until the mixture is coated. Add the eggs, vanilla, marmalade, and rum. Mix well until combined. Scrape the mixture into the prepared mold and cover securely with the lid.

Fill a large stockpot with about 2 in/5 cm of water. Fit the pot with a vegetable steamer basket and bring the water to a simmer. Bring extra water to a boil in a teakettle.

Set the pudding mold on the steamer basket and add boiling water until the water level in the stockpot reaches about a third up the sides of the pudding mold. Cover the pot and cook the pudding at a simmer for 6 hours. Check the water every so often to make sure that it hasn't boiled off. Add more hot water as needed.

When the pudding is done, it will be set and the top will be dark brown. Carefully remove the mold from the pot, uncover, and place on a wire rack to cool for 30 minutes. (If you are serving the pudding the same day, unmold it onto a plate and make the sauce. If you are preparing the pudding ahead and want to cure it, keep the pudding in the mold, let it cool completely, and refrigerate for up to 1 week. The day you plan to serve it, steam it for 2 hours, as directed.)

TO MAKE THE HARD SAUCE / In the bowl of a stand mixer fitted with the whisk attachment, beat the butter on medium-high speed until light and fluffy, about 2 minutes. Add the brown sugar and beat for 2 minutes. Add the rum and beat for 1 minute more, until combined. Scrape mixture into a small bowl, cover with plastic wrap, and refrigerate for at least 1 hour or up to 3 days.

Place the chilled sauce in a bowl and serve with the unmolded pudding. The sauce is designed to be spread like butter on slices of the pudding.

04

PIES & TARTS

PIES TO ME MEAN HOME, HEARTH, AND FAMILY.

There's something special about having a pie on the counter, ready for snacking or dessert. My family is somewhat unorthodox when it comes to breakfast foods, so we often have leftover pie for breakfast. Heaven! Of course, pie is excellent with a dollop of ice cream after a holiday meal or in the afternoon as a pick-me-up. And pies are so versatile—you can put just about any filling you want into them.

In this chapter, I include traditional pies for the Thanksgiving season: pumpkin, apple, and maple-pecan. The Pumpkin Pie easily can be converted to a Sweet Potato Pie, making it appropriate for Kwanzaa. I also offer a version of the traditional English Christmas treat, Mincemeat Tarts. And, finally, I developed a truly out-of-this-world, special pie, the Chocolate–Sunflower Butter Pie, in honor of Kwanzaa.

PUMPKIN PIE

Flaky Pie Crust (page 108)

2 extra-large eggs, at room temperature

½ cup/105 g packed dark brown sugar

1 tsp ground cinnamon

½ tsp ground ginger

1 tsp salt

1½ cups/360 ml evaporated milk

15-oz/430-g can pumpkin purée or 1¾ cups/420 ml sweet potato purée

2 Tbsp unsalted butter, melted

Unsweetened whipped cream (optional)

Every year, we spend Thanksgiving with my daughter's best friend and his parents. One of the most anticipated parts of the dinner is the pumpkin pie for dessert. Even though everyone originally came to the table with different expectations of what pumpkin pie should taste like, they all love this version. It goes a bit lighter on the spices than do other recipes, which allows the flavor of the pumpkin—or the sweet potato—to shine through. The inspiration for this pie came from one of my favorite vegetarian cookbooks, *The Tao of Cooking* by Sally Pasley.

Line a 9-in/23-cm pie pan with the crust dough. Refrigerate until needed. (Freeze the remaining dough for later use.)

Preheat the oven to 450°F/230°C/gas mark 8.

In a large bowl, whisk the eggs until foamy. Whisk in the brown sugar, cinnamon, ginger, and salt. Whisk in the evaporated milk. Stir in the pumpkin purée and mix well. Add the butter and mix until smooth and uniform.

Remove the lined pan from the refrigerator and pour in the filling. Place the pan in the oven, immediately reduce the temperature to 375°/190°C/gas mark 5, and bake until a toothpick inserted into the middle of the pie comes out fairly clean (not goopy), 60 to 75 minutes.

Place the pie on a wire rack to cool to room temperature and allow the custard to set. Serve wedges of the pie with whipped cream (if using).

 APPLE-CINNAMON PIE

Flaky Pie Crust (page 108)

6 large, firm but ripe apples of your choice, peeled, cored, and thinly sliced

½ cup/105 g packed dark brown sugar

3 Tbsp Jeanne's Gluten-Free All-Purpose Flour (page 17)

¼ tsp salt

1 tsp ground cinnamon

⅛ tsp freshly grated nutmeg

1 tsp grated lemon zest

2 Tbsp cold unsalted butter, cut into small pieces

1 extra-large egg whisked with 1 Tbsp of water, for egg wash (optional)

Granulated sugar for sprinkling (optional)

8 TO 10 SERVINGS Apple pie is the one pie I make year-round. There are always fresh apples at the market, and I like to try different varieties and to mix and match them. I like to use a mixture of tart, perfumy, and sweet apples. I grow Honeycrisp and Liberty apples in my garden, so I often use those together, along with Gala apples. But everyone seems to have their own favorite combinations. There really isn't a best one. That said, an apple I do not recommend for pie is the Red Delicious—it gets mealy when cooked. You can jazz up the pie a bit by adding ¼ cup/30 g cranberries to the apple filling. The pleasing tartness of the cranberries will be nicely offset by the sweetness of the apples.

Line a 9-in/23-cm pie pan with the crust dough. Refrigerate until needed.

Preheat the oven to 450°F/230°C/gas mark 8.

Place the apples in a large bowl. Add the brown sugar, flour, salt, cinnamon, nutmeg, and lemon zest and mix with a large spoon to combine—be sure that all the apple slices are covered with the mixture.

Roll out the dough for the top crust. Remove the lined pan from the refrigerator and pour in the filling. Dot with the butter pieces. Place the dough over the filling, seal and cut air vents as directed on page 109. Brush with the egg wash and sprinkle with granulated sugar (if using).

Bake the pie for 10 minutes. Reduce the oven temperature to 350°F/180°C/gas mark 4 and continue to bake until the crust is brown and the apples are tender when pierced with a small, sharp knife through one of the air vents, 30 to 45 minutes. You want the crust to be golden brown but not burnt—start watching it at about 30 minutes.

Place the pie on a wire rack to cool. Serve warm or at room temperature.

MAPLE-PECAN PIE

8 TO 10 SERVINGS

Pecan pie is one of my very favorite pies. This pie is extra special because it uses maple syrup instead of corn syrup as a sweetener. Maple goes very well with pecans. And the smell of this pie as it's baking is truly out of this world. I like to use grade B syrup—it's more flavorful than other grades. To make this pie a Chocolate-Pecan Pie, add 1 cup/170 g semisweet chocolate chips to the lined pan along with the pecans, then pour the maple syrup filling on top.

Flaky Pie Crust (page 108)

2 cups/240 g coarsely chopped pecans

1 cup/240 ml maple syrup, preferably grade B

¾ cup/160 g packed dark brown sugar

3 extra-large eggs, at room temperature

1 Tbsp unsalted butter, melted and cooled

1 Tbsp Jeanne's Gluten-Free All-Purpose Flour (page 17)

1 tsp pure vanilla extract

¼ tsp salt

Unsweetened whipped cream (optional)

Line a 9-in/23-cm pie pan with the crust dough. Refrigerate until needed. (Freeze the remaining dough for later use.)

Preheat the oven to 350°F/180°C/gas mark 4.

In a medium frying pan over medium heat, toast the pecans, stirring often, until they give off a nice fragrance and are a darker brown, 3 to 5 minutes. Let cool.

In a large bowl, whisk together the maple syrup, brown sugar, eggs, butter, flour, vanilla, and salt until smooth.

Remove the lined pan from the refrigerator. Evenly spread the toasted pecans on the bottom and pour the maple syrup mixture over the top. Carefully set the pan in the oven. (You may want to place a cookie sheet on the rack beneath the pie to catch any drips.)

Bake until the filling is puffed and set, about 60 minutes. Place the pie on a wire rack to cool. Serve wedges of the pie topped with whipped cream (if using).

CHOCOLATE-SUNFLOWER BUTTER PIE

CRUST

1½ cups/210 g Jeanne's Gluten-Free All-Purpose Flour (page 17)

¼ cup/20 g unsweetened cocoa powder, sifted

½ cup/100 g granulated sugar

½ tsp salt

½ cup/115 g cold unsalted butter, cut into pieces

2 Tbsp heavy cream

½ tsp pure vanilla extract

FILLING

8 oz/225 g cream cheese, at room temperature

2 Tbsp unsalted butter, melted and cooled slightly

1 cup/200 g granulated sugar

1 cup/270 g sunflower seed butter such as SunButter

1 cup/240 ml heavy cream

1 Tbsp pure vanilla extract

GANACHE

½ cup/120 ml heavy cream

⅔ cup/115 g semisweet chocolate chips

8 TO 10 SERVINGS This pie always gets rave reviews when I serve it. It's reminiscent of a chocolate–peanut butter cup. This pie has two ingredients with African roots: chocolate and sunflower seeds. Sunflower seed butter is something I discovered when my daughter was diagnosed with a life-threatening peanut allergy. For a Chocolate–Peanut Butter Pie, you can substitute peanut butter.

TO MAKE THE CRUST / Grease and flour a 10-in/25.4-cm pie pan, preferably glass or ceramic. Place the flour, cocoa powder, sugar, and salt in a food processor. Pulse a few times to combine. Add the butter and pulse several times until the mixture looks like wet pebbles. Add the cream and vanilla and pulse until the mixture starts to come together and looks like coarse meal. (You can also mix the dough in a bowl with a pastry cutter.) Put the dough in the prepared pan and press onto the bottom and up the sides. The crust should reach just to the top of the sides and not cover the rim. Refrigerate the lined pan for 15 minutes. Preheat the oven to 350°F/180°C/gas mark 4.

Remove the lined pan from the refrigerator and, with a fork, prick the bottom all over. Bake until the crust is a bit more brown, about 15 minutes. Remove to a wire rack to cool completely.

TO MAKE THE FILLING / In the bowl of a stand mixer fitted with the paddle attachment, beat the cream cheese on medium speed until fluffy, about 2 minutes. Reduce the speed to low, add the butter, and beat to combine. Increase the speed to medium, add the sugar, and beat for 2 minutes. Add the sunflower seed butter and beat for 1 minute.

In a separate large bowl, using a hand mixer on medium-high speed or a whisk, beat the cream until it forms stiff peaks. Add the vanilla and beat to combine. Add ¼ cup/60 ml of the cream cheese mixture to the whipped cream and whisk to combine. Add the remaining cream cheese mixture and, using a rubber spatula, fold together until combined. Scrape the filling into the crust and refrigerate for 30 minutes.

TO MAKE THE GANACHE / In a small saucepan, heat the cream over low heat until just boiling. Remove from the heat, add the chocolate chips, and let sit for 1 minute. Whisk until the chocolate is melted and the mixture is smooth, then let cool a bit. You want the ganache to be warm (not hot) and thick but still fairly pourable.

Remove the chilled pie from the refrigerator and carefully pour the ganache over the middle of the pie. Smooth the ganache toward the edges, but leave a 1-in/2.5-cm border uncovered. Return the pie to the refrigerator for at least 1 hour before serving to let the filling and ganache set.

Store, tightly covered, in the refrigerator for up to 3 days.

MINCEMEAT TARTS

24 BITE-SIZE TARTS Mincemeat tarts are a traditional treat during English Christmas celebrations. The filling originally contained dried fruits mixed with beef and beef suet, hence the name, "minced meat" tarts. Nowadays, the tarts are often made without beef and with butter or shortening instead of suet. Not only are these mini tarts surprisingly good, but they are charming adorned on top with a star-shaped pastry. If you like, you can make the filling in advance and store in the refrigerator for up to 5 days, which allows the flavors to meld.

Put the apple, raisins, figs, cherries, ginger, brown sugar, butter, brandy, orange zest, lemon zest, cinnamon, nutmeg, allspice, and cloves in a food processor. Pulse about 12 times. Or, you can chop the ingredients by hand, place in a bowl, and then stir in the brandy. The ingredients should be chopped finely and be fairly uniform, but you can chop or process them to your preferred level of coarseness.

Preheat the oven to 400°F/200°C/gas mark 6.

Have ready a 24-cup mini-muffin pan. Remove one crust dough disk from the refrigerator. Place between two sheets of waxed paper and roll to 1/8 in/3 mm thick (no thinner). Using a round 2½-in/6.5-cm cookie cutter, cut out as many rounds as you can. Place each round over a mini-muffin cup and gently press it into the cup. I've found that it's best to press the middle and then the sides. If the dough breaks, just smooth it to fix or add a bit of dough to the broken part. When you cut out more rounds from the scraps and from the

second dough disk, place the muffin pan in the refrigerator. This helps keep the crusts flaky when baked. You will use only part of the second disk (save the remainder for later). When you have filled the 24 cups, with the tines of a fork, press along the edges of the dough in each cup to give them a decorative edge.

Stir the filling to distribute the liquid. Fill each lined cup with 1 Tbsp filling, and return the pan to the refrigerator. Roll out the remaining dough to 1/8 in/3 mm thick. Using a 1½-in/4-cm star cookie cutter, cut out 24 stars. Remove the pan from the refrigerator. Top each tart with a star. Brush the top of each tart with the egg wash and sprinkle with granulated sugar (if using).

Bake until the star crust is golden and the filling is bubbling, 15 to 20 minutes. Let the tarts cool in the pan on a wire rack for 10 minutes, then carefully remove to the rack to cool completely.

Store in an airtight container at room temperature for up to 5 days.

½ apple with skin, cored

½ cup/75 g raisins

½ cup/30 g dried figs, chopped

¼ cup/40 g dried cherries or cranberries

1 Tbsp crystallized ginger, chopped

3 Tbsp packed dark brown sugar

1 Tbsp cold unsalted butter

2 Tbsp brandy, rum, marsala, or apple juice

¾ tsp grated orange zest

¾ tsp grated lemon zest

¼ tsp ground cinnamon

Pinch of freshly grated nutmeg

Pinch of ground allspice

Pinch of ground cloves

Flaky Pie Crust (page 108)

1 extra-large egg beaten with 1 Tbsp water, for egg wash (optional)

Granulated sugar for sprinkling (optional)

FLAKY
PIE CRUST

1 DOUBLE CRUST FOR A 9- OR 10-IN/23- OR 25-CM PIE

2⅓ cups/325 g Jeanne's Gluten-Free All-Purpose Flour (page 17)

1 Tbsp granulated sugar

¼ tsp salt

1 cup/225 g cold unsalted butter, lard, margarine, or shortening, or a combination, cut into pieces

1 Tbsp vinegar such as apple cider

4 to 7 Tbsp ice water

Tapioca flour for dusting

Pie crust seems to inspire fear in folks who have never made it before. I'm not sure why, because pie dough is one of the most forgiving doughs to work with. Gluten-free dough is actually ahead of the game—there is no gluten to overdevelop and make the final crust tough. It always turns out flaky! One thing to keep in mind is that you want to keep the dough cool at all times. If the dough gets too warm, it starts to become floppy and unworkable. Just follow the directions and you'll be fine—I promise!

The instructions here are for rolling out the dough on a floured surface. But if you have too much trouble rolling or transferring the dough with a rolling pin, roll it between sheets of waxed paper. Then remove the top sheet and invert the pie pan on the dough. Holding the pan with one hand and the dough with the other, turn the pan and dough together and flip the dough onto the pan. Remove the paper and gently press the dough in place.

In a large bowl, mix together the all-purpose flour, sugar, and salt. Add the butter pieces and, with your fingers, start rubbing the butter and dry ingredients together until the mixture looks like wet sand mixed with pebbles of various sizes. This will take a bit of time, but work as quickly as possible so the butter does not warm up too much. You don't want the butter to start melting. I like to do this by hand to get a feel for the dough. You can also do this initial mixing with a food processor.

Add the vinegar and rub into the mixture. Add the ice water, 1 Tbsp at a time, rubbing it into the mixture. You want to add enough water to create a dough that holds together well, but isn't wet. How much you will need depends on the humidity of your kitchen.

Divide the dough into two fairly equal pieces, shape into disks, and wrap each tightly in plastic wrap. Refrigerate for about 30 minutes or up to 3 days.

When you are ready to roll out the dough, dust your rolling surface well with tapioca flour. Also flour your rolling pin. Remove one dough disk from the refrigerator, place on the floured surface, and sprinkle with tapioca flour. The key to successfully rolling out gluten-free pie dough is to go slow. When I say slow, I mean *slow*. And use a light touch. If your dough starts cracking, slow down and don't press so hard with your rolling pin. Also, stop and fix the cracks—the dough is forgiving. Carefully and patiently roll out the dough into a 10- to 11-in/25- to 28-cm circle

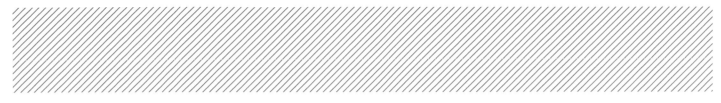

(big enough to fit your pie pan). If the dough sticks to the rolling pin, add more tapioca flour.

Keep in mind that the dough should be cool but not too cold. It should roll fairly easily and should not break too much. If the dough seems too cold and you have to work hard to roll it, step back and let it warm up a bit before you continue. If the dough looks as if it's "sweating" and is almost squishy, it is too warm and should be refrigerated a bit longer.

Next, you are going to use the rolling pin to transport the dough to the pie pan. Sprinkle tapioca flour over the entire surface of the dough. Put the rolling pin near an edge of the dough round. Again, go slowly! Roll the dough around the rolling pin until all the dough is on the pin. The dough should roll easily without breaking. If it breaks, you can easily fix the breaks by pinching the dough together. (Again, if the dough tears all over the place, it's a bit too cold. Step away and let the dough warm up slightly before proceeding.)

Lift the pin with the dough and put near the side of the pie pan. Unroll the dough onto the pan so it is covered evenly. Carefully and slowly press the dough into place, starting with the middle bottom of the pan and working out to the bottom edges and then up the sides. When you get to the rim, press the dough onto the rim. Finally, press down and carefully tear off any leftover dough. Set these scraps aside—you may use them later. Refrigerate the lined pan while you prepare the filling for the pie.

If the pie requires a top crust, roll out the remaining dough in the same way. Remove the pie pan from the refrigerator and place the filling inside as directed in the recipe. Roll the dough for the top crust onto your rolling pin and unroll over the pie filling. Carefully press the top and bottom edges together around the rim to form a seal. You can create a decorative edge by pinching the dough together with the thumb and forefinger of one hand and the forefinger of the other hand. Or, you can carefully press down along the rim with the tines of a fork. Be sure you've created a good seal— any unsealed portion will cause filling to leak onto the floor of your oven during baking. (You may want to place a cookie sheet on the bottom rack of your oven to catch any filling.) With a sharp knife, make a few short slashes in the top to create air vents. These will allow steam to escape. I like to make four short cuts in the middle.

If you are so inclined, roll out the dough scraps and cut out cute designs to put on top of the pie. For example, for an apple pie I might cut out an apple with a stem and a leaf.

If you are making a single-crust pie, the remaining dough disk, wrapped tightly in plastic wrap, may be frozen for up to 3 months. To defrost, let the frozen disk stand in the refrigerator for 24 hours. Remove from the refrigerator, and when the dough has reached rolling temperature, roll out and shape as directed.

Bake the pie as directed.

05

BREADS & CRACKERS

BREAD IS A FUNDAMENTAL FOOD. Many people assume that since I can't eat gluten, I can't eat bread. Sometimes I think that they pity me a bit. But no pity is needed! I bake and eat many kinds of bread, including biscuits, rolls, and crackers. The sky's the limit as far as I'm concerned. When it comes to specialty holiday breads, I usually have my wheat-eating friends at a disadvantage because my repertoire has tried-and-true recipes for items that are hard for them to find at the store.

In this chapter, you'll find basics like sandwich bread, rolls, biscuits, and cornbread. I also include breads specific to the season: St. Lucia Buns, Panettone, and Stollen. I share some extras such as Date Nut Bread that my family likes to enjoy around Thanksgiving and are appropriate for Kwanzaa. Cheese Crackers and Straws are fabulous for New Year's parties.

SIMPLE SCONES

I like to make these scones on weekend or holiday mornings because they are quick to mix and bake. The scones have a lightly crunchy exterior, with a fluffy and buttery crumb inside. The butter gives them a richness that makes them melt in your mouth. You have the option of keeping them fairly plain or adding your favorite extras, like currants for more traditional scones, or nuts for crunchy scones, or chocolate chips for a decadent treat. Whether or not you make the scones plain or with additions, they are nice spread with jam (yes, even the chocolate ones—which I like with marmalade).

Preheat the oven to 400°F/200°C/ gas mark 6. Line a cookie sheet with parchment paper.

In the bowl of a stand mixer fitted with the paddle attachment, beat the flour, baking powder, baking soda, salt, sugar, and lemon zest for a few seconds to combine. Add the butter pieces and beat until the mixture looks like wet sand with pebbles, about 1 minute. Add the currants (if using) and beat for a few seconds to combine. Add the 1 cup/240 ml cream and beat for a few seconds, just until the dough sticks together.

Remove the dough from the bowl and press together with your hands into a cohesive ball. Work quickly so the dough doesn't get too warm. Place the dough on the prepared sheet, cover with a piece of waxed paper, and roll to a circle that is ½ to ¾ in/12 mm to 2 cm thick (no thinner) and about 9 in/23 cm in diameter. Remove the waxed paper and tidy up the edges with your hands. Using a sharp knife, cut the dough into 12 wedges. I recommend making an initial cut from top to bottom, and then another cut from side to side, dividing the circle into equal quarters. Then, cut 3 equal wedges from each quarter. Keep the wedges in the circle form. Lightly brush the tops with the 1 Tbsp cream.

Bake until the scones have risen and are lightly golden on top, 15 to 20 minutes. Let cool in the pan. Serve warm or at room temperature.

Store in an airtight container at room temperature for up to 5 days.

2 cups/280 g Jeanne's Gluten-Free All-Purpose Flour (page 17)

4 tsp baking powder

½ tsp baking soda

½ tsp salt

⅓ cup/65 g granulated sugar

1 tsp grated lemon or orange zest

6 Tbsp/85 g cold unsalted butter, cut into 12 pieces

½ cup/60 g dried currants or toasted pecans or ½ cup/80 g chocolate chips (optional)

1 cup/240 ml cold heavy cream, plus 1 Tbsp heavy cream

ST. LUCIA BUNS

¼ to ½ tsp saffron threads

¼ cup/55 g unsalted butter, melted and cooled a bit

1 Tbsp granulated sugar plus ¼ cup/50 g

1½ cups/360 ml warm milk (about 110°F/43°C)

2 Tbsp active dry yeast

3 cups/420 g Jeanne's Gluten-Free All-Purpose Flour (page 17)

2 tsp xanthan gum

4 tsp baking powder

1 tsp salt

2 extra-large eggs, at room temperature, plus 1 extra-large egg beaten with 2 Tbsp milk, for egg wash

2 tsp vinegar, preferably apple cider

½ tsp pure vanilla extract

Tapioca flour for sprinkling

Raisins for decorating

In Sweden, December 13 is St. Lucia's Day. According to the old Julian calendar, this was also the winter solstice and was celebrated with a festival of lights. Nowadays, it marks the beginning of the Christmas season in Sweden. Saffron is used in St. Lucia buns, or *lussebullar*, to give them a bright yellow color symbolizing the light that, in ancient times, kept demons at bay during the darkest period of the year. On this day, the mother of the house is treated to breakfast in bed and served hot coffee along with the buns. In schools, one or more lucky girls are chosen to represent St. Lucia. They dress in white robes and wear a wreath of candles (nowadays electric) in their hair. The buns are traditionally formed into various shapes, including crowns and cats. Here, I offer another traditional shape—a backward S decorated with raisins. The buns are rich and sweet, with a moist interior scented with saffron.

Line two cookie sheets with parchment paper.

In a small bowl, crumble the saffron threads into the melted butter and stir. Let sit for about 15 minutes to allow the saffron to permeate the butter.

In a small bowl, whisk the 1 Tbsp sugar into the warm milk until dissolved. Whisk in the yeast until dissolved. Set aside to proof. The mixture will get foamy. If your kitchen is warm, the mixture may foam quickly—watch it to make sure it doesn't overflow the bowl.

In a medium bowl, mix together the all-purpose flour, xanthan gum, baking powder, salt, and ¼ cup/50 g sugar.

In the bowl of a stand mixer fitted with the paddle attachment, beat the whole eggs, vinegar, vanilla, and saffron-infused butter on low speed to combine. Add the yeast mixture and beat briefly to combine. Add the flour mixture and beat briefly to combine, then increase the speed to medium-high and beat for 3 minutes longer.

Sprinkle tapioca flour over your rolling surface. Dust your hands with tapioca flour. Pull off a ⅓-cup/75-ml chunk of dough and roll into a ball. Place on the rolling surface and roll into a uniform, thick log about 8 in/ 20 cm long. Brush off the extra tapioca flour with a pastry brush. Place the log on a prepared sheet and form into a tightly coiled backward S shape. Press lightly on the top and bottom of the S toward the middle to make sure the ends are sticking to the body of the S. Press a raisin in the middle of the coil at each end. Repeat until all the dough is used, spacing the buns 1-in/2.5-cm apart on the sheets.

Preheat the oven to 375°F/190°C/gas mark 5.

CONTINUED /

Let the buns stand in a warm, draft-free place to rise until double in bulk, 45 to 60 minutes. (I usually do this on top of the stove while the oven is preheating.)

Lightly brush the top of each bun with the egg wash. You may dislodge the raisins—just put them back into position. Bake until the buns are golden brown on top, about 20 minutes. Remove to wire racks to cool.

The buns are best eaten the day they are baked but can be stored in an airtight container at room temperature for up to 7 days. Microwave stored buns for a few seconds to refresh the texture.

APPLESAUCE SPICE MUFFINS

18 MUFFINS Everyone gets pretty busy and feels hectic during the holidays. I like to have a portable snack on hand, and these muffins fit the bill. They are also delicious for a quick breakfast on the go. I keep applesauce in the pantry, making the muffins easy to whip up whenever I need them. The muffins are nicely sweet and very moist, due to the applesauce.

Preheat the oven to 350°F/180°C/gas mark 4. Grease 18 standard muffin cups (one 12-cup pan and one 6-cup pan) with butter and dust with tapioca flour, or line the cups with paper liners.

In a large bowl, mix together the all-purpose flour, baking soda, baking powder, salt, cinnamon, cloves, and allspice.

In the bowl of a stand mixer fitted with the paddle attachment, beat the butter and sugar on medium-high speed until light and fluffy, about 1 minute. Add the eggs, one at a time, beating after each addition. Then beat for 2 minutes longer. Add the applesauce and beat to combine—the mixture will look curdled and that's okay. Reduce the speed to medium and add the flour mixture alternately with the buttermilk in small batches, beginning and ending with the flour. Beat until just combined. With a spoon, stir in the nuts.

Spoon the dough into the prepared muffin cups, filling them three-fourths full.

Bake until a toothpick inserted into the middle of a muffin comes out clean, about 25 minutes. Turn out onto wire racks to cool.

Store in an airtight container at room temperature for up to 5 days.

½ cup/115 g unsalted butter, at room temperature, plus more for greasing

Tapioca flour for dusting

2½ cups/350 g Jeanne's Gluten-Free All-Purpose Flour (page 17)

1½ tsp baking soda

1 tsp baking powder

½ tsp salt

¾ tsp ground cinnamon

½ tsp ground cloves

½ tsp ground allspice

1¼ cups/250 g granulated sugar

2 extra-large eggs, at room temperature

1½ cups/360 ml applesauce

½ cup/120 ml buttermilk

1 cup/115 g coarsely chopped walnuts or pecans

CINNAMON ROLLS

I married a man who loves cinnamon rolls. And our daughter loves them, too. Since I can't eat commercial cinnamon rolls, I developed this recipe, which has all the hallmarks of what I consider to be a perfect cinnamon roll: light bread, cinnamon filling, and cream cheese frosting. If you don't have a large rectangular baking pan, you can use two 8-in/20-cm square pans and arrange six rolls in each.

FILLING

¼ cup/55 g unsalted butter, at room temperature

¾ cup/160 g packed dark brown sugar

2 Tbsp Jeanne's Gluten-Free All-Purpose Flour (page 17)

1 tsp ground cinnamon

Melted unsalted butter for brushing

Tapioca flour for dusting

3 cups/420 g Jeanne's Gluten-Free All-Purpose Flour (page 17)

2 tsp xanthan gum

4 tsp baking powder

1 tsp salt

4 Tbsp/50 g granulated sugar

1¼ cups/300 ml warm milk (about 110°F/43°C)

2 Tbsp active dry yeast

2 extra-large eggs

¼ cup/60 ml neutral-tasting oil such as rice bran or canola

2 tsp vinegar, preferably apple cider

TO MAKE THE FILLING / Combine the butter, brown sugar, all-purpose flour, and cinnamon in a small saucepan. Cook over low heat, stirring, until the butter melts. Watch carefully so the mixture doesn't burn. Remove from the heat and put aside.

Brush a 9-by-13-in/23-by-33-cm baking pan with melted butter and dust with tapioca flour.

In a medium bowl, mix together the all-purpose flour, xanthan gum, baking powder, salt, and 3 Tbsp of the sugar. In a small bowl, whisk the remaining 1 Tbsp sugar into the milk until dissolved. Whisk in the yeast until dissolved. Set aside to proof. The mixture will get foamy. If your kitchen is warm, the mixture may foam quickly—watch it to make sure it doesn't overflow the bowl.

In the bowl of a stand mixer fitted with the paddle attachment, beat the eggs, oil, and vinegar on low speed until just combined. Add the yeast mixture and beat for a few seconds to combine. Add the flour mixture and beat briefly to combine. Increase the speed to high and beat for 3 minutes longer. The dough will be very stiff and sticky.

Spread a large piece of plastic wrap—at least 12 by 18 in/30.5 by 46 cm—on your rolling surface. Generously dust with tapioca flour. The plastic wrap should be completely covered. Scrape the dough onto the floured surface. Liberally sprinkle the dough and a rolling pin with tapioca flour. Roll the dough to a 12-by-15-in/30.5-by-38-cm rectangle (you can use your fingers to push it out here and there into the correct shape). It will be about ¼ in/6 mm thick. Sprinkle the filling over the dough, leaving a ½-in/12-mm border uncovered on the two long sides and one short side, and a 1-in/2.5-cm border uncovered on the other short side. You may have to work a bit to cover the dough. I use a butter knife to scrape the filling over the dough.

With a pastry brush, brush the 1-in/2.5-cm border of dough on the short side with water. This will help seal the rolls. Starting at the short side with the ½-in/12-mm border, carefully roll the dough into a fairly tight cylinder. This should be easy if you adequately floured your work surface. If the dough sticks, gently pick up the end of the plastic wrap and use it to help push and roll the dough. When you reach the side brushed with water, press it carefully but firmly onto the body of the cylinder. You should have a cylinder 12 in/30.5 cm long. Don't worry if it's a bit longer or shorter. You can pat the ends a bit with your hands to make them more even.

Sprinkle more tapioca flour on your work surface. Carefully pick up the cylinder and place it in the middle of the floured surface. Starting at one end, and using a ruler and a sharp knife, mark the dough in 1-in/2.5-cm increments. You should have 11 marks. Carefully cut the dough at the marks. I wipe off the knife after each cut. Place each roll, cut-side up, in the prepared pan. The 12 rolls should be slightly touching but will have a bit of room around them. The rolls bake best if not tightly squished together.

Preheat the oven to 375°F/190°C/gas mark 5.

Cover the rolls lightly with plastic wrap and let stand in a warm, draft-free place until nearly double in bulk, 30 to 40 minutes. (I usually do this on top of the stove while the oven is preheating.)

Remove the plastic wrap and brush the tops of the rolls with melted butter. Bake until the tops are tinged brown here and there but are not totally brown, 35 to 40 minutes. Let cool in the pan on a wire rack.

MEANWHILE, TO MAKE THE FROSTING / In a small bowl, combine the butter, cream cheese, confectioners' sugar, and vanilla. Using a hand mixer on medium speed, beat until combined and smooth.

Brush the frosting on the rolls while they are in the pan. The warmer the rolls are, the more the frosting will melt into the rolls and not stay on top (which isn't necessarily a bad thing. I usually frost some rolls and leave others plain.)

The rolls are best eaten the day they are made. They may be stored in an airtight container at room temperature for up to 3 days. Microwave for a few seconds to refresh the texture.

FROSTING

¼ cup/55 g unsalted butter, at room temperature

4 oz/115 g cream cheese, at room temperature

¾ cup/85 g confectioners' sugar, sifted

½ tsp pure vanilla extract

DINNER ROLLS

18 ROLLS Every Thanksgiving while I was growing up, my mom made Parker House rolls. The rolls had a terrific taste and texture—they were soft and cushy, and a bit sweet, and had butter-brushed tops. I carried on the tradition when I moved out and started hosting my own Thanksgiving dinners. Of course, I had to come up with a gluten-free version as good as my mom's rolls. And I've succeeded. This recipe for the rolls elicits swoons of pleasure from people who eat them!

Melted unsalted butter for brushing

Tapioca flour for dusting

4 Tbsp/50 g granulated sugar

2 cups/480 ml warm milk (about 110°F/43°C)

2 Tbsp active dry yeast

3 cups/420 g Jeanne's Gluten-Free All-Purpose Flour (page 17)

2 tsp xanthan gum

4 tsp baking powder

1 tsp salt

2 extra-large eggs

¼ cup/60 ml neutral-flavored oil such as rice bran or canola

2 tsp vinegar, preferably apple cider

Brush 18 standard muffin cups (one 12-cup pan and one 6-cup pan) with melted butter and dust with tapioca flour.

In a small bowl, whisk 1 Tbsp of the sugar into the warm milk. Whisk in the yeast to dissolve. Set aside to proof. The mixture will get foamy. If your kitchen is warm, the mixture will foam quickly—watch it to make sure it doesn't overflow the bowl.

In a medium bowl, mix together the all-purpose flour, xanthan gum, baking powder, salt, and remaining 3 Tbsp sugar.

In the bowl of stand mixer fitted with the paddle attachment, beat the eggs on medium speed until foamy, about 3 minutes. Add the oil and beat for 2 minutes. Reduce the speed to low, add the vinegar, and beat to combine. Add the yeast mixture and beat to mix. Add the flour mixture and beat to combine, then increase the speed to medium-high and beat for 3 minutes longer.

Distribute the dough equally among the prepared muffin cups, filling them about three-fourths full. With a sharp knife that has been dipped in tapioca flour, cut a deep slash in the top of each roll. Dip the knife in flour before each cut, and don't worry if a little extra tapioca flour is left on top of the rolls.

Preheat the oven to 375°F/190°C/gas mark 5.

Let the dough stand in a warm, draft-free place to rise until doubled in bulk, about 40 minutes. (I usually do this on top of the stove while the oven is preheating.)

Brush the top of each roll with melted butter. Bake until the tops are a nice golden brown, about 20 minutes. If they start to brown too quickly, loosely tent the rolls with aluminum foil. Remove the rolls to wire racks to cool. If you are serving them immediately, it's nice to put them in a tea towel–lined basket to keep warm.

Store in an airtight container at room temperature for up to 3 days.

FEATHERLIGHT
BUTTERMILK BISCUITS

1 DOZEN BISCUITS This recipe is adapted from one by Shirley O. Corriher, a biochemist who is among my food goddesses. I have learned a great deal from her books, *BakeWise* and *CookWise*. She explains why things work the way they do in baking and cooking. I had the honor of attending a demonstration where Shirley explained her biscuit recipe. She told us that the key to light, fluffy biscuits is a wet dough. The water in the dough turns into steam and helps puff out the biscuits. I immediately came home and adapted her recipe and technique, and she is right! These are the lightest and most delectable biscuits I have ever eaten. Truly worth the name "featherlight."

Melted unsalted butter for brushing, plus ¼ cup/55 g cold unsalted butter, cut into pieces

2 cups/280 g Jeanne's Gluten-Free All-Purpose Flour (page 17), sifted

1 Tbsp baking powder

½ tsp baking soda

½ tsp salt

¼ cup/50 g granulated sugar

⅔ cup/165 ml heavy cream

¾ cup/180 ml buttermilk

1 cup/120 g tapioca flour

Preheat the oven to 425°F/220°C/gas mark 7. Brush a 9-in/23-cm round cake pan with melted butter.

In a large bowl, mix together the all-purpose flour, baking powder, baking soda, salt, and sugar. Rub in the cold butter pieces with your fingers until the mixture looks like a pebbles of different sizes. With a large spoon, gently stir in the cream, then the buttermilk. The dough should be wet and resemble cottage cheese.

Place the tapioca flour in a medium bowl. Scoop out ¼ cup/60 ml of the dough and form into a ball. Place the ball in the tapioca flour and roll in the flour until covered. Shake off the excess flour by tossing the ball back and forth between your hands a few times.

Set the dough ball along the edge of the prepared pan. Repeat with the remaining dough, placing each ball next to the previous one. Once the perimeter of the pan is filled with nine balls, arrange the remaining three balls in the middle. All the biscuits should be touching each other. They will be misshapen—don't worry, they will puff out in the oven.

Bake until the biscuits are lightly browned, 25 to 30 minutes. Remove from the oven and brush the biscuits with melted butter. Carefully invert onto a plate and then onto another, so the biscuits are right-side up. With a knife, cut between the biscuits before serving.

Store in an airtight container at room temperature for up to 3 days.

SKILLET
CORNBREAD

Southern food is some of my favorite American regional food ever. I try hard to be true to my imaginary Southern roots, but there is one place where I fail miserably: I put sugar in my cornbread. Yes, I admit it. I have a sweet tooth. I have friends who are Southern girls, and they refuse even to look at me if I put sugar in the cornbread I serve them. So I developed this recipe to make everyone happy: you get to choose how much sugar you want to use. Since the bread is easy to make, you can bake a batch to eat and another batch to cut into cubes for Thanksgiving dressing or stuffing.

2 Tbsp unsalted butter

1 cup /130 g gluten-free corn flour such as masa harina

1 cup/160 g gluten-free cornmeal, preferably medium grind

2 tsp baking powder

½ tsp baking soda

½ tsp salt

2 tsp to ¼ cup/50 g granulated sugar (optional)

2 extra-large eggs, at room temperature

¾ cup/170 g yogurt or sour cream

¾ cup/180 ml milk

Preheat the oven to 425°F/220°C/gas mark 7. When the oven is heated to temperature, place the butter in a 10-in/25-cm cast-iron skillet and slip the skillet in the oven to heat the pan and melt the butter.

Meanwhile, in a large bowl, mix together the corn flour, cornmeal, baking powder, baking soda, and salt. Stir in the amount of sugar you want or no sugar at all. In a medium bowl, whisk together the eggs, yogurt, and milk until fairly smooth. Add the egg mixture to the cornmeal mixture and mix with a large spoon until combined.

Carefully remove the hot skillet from the oven. Carefully swirl the butter around the skillet to make sure it covers the bottom of the pan. Pour the batter into the skillet.

Bake until the cornbread is firm and the top is golden brown, about 20 minutes. The top will have cracked a bit—that's fine. Let the cornbread cool in the skillet on top of stove. Cut into wedges to serve.

The bread is best within 2 days after baking. Store in an airtight container at room temperature for up to 3 days.

SOFT SANDWICH BREAD

1 LOAF This is a perfect everyday bread. It's soft, and it stays fresh in taste and texture for days. I bake several loaves during the holidays to have on hand for toast and sandwiches. It's particularly nice used for after-Thanksgiving turkey sandwiches. The bread is also terrific for making bread crumbs and croutons, and as the basis for Stuffing Like Mama Made (page 134). And, it's ideal for French toast on cold winter mornings.

Brush a 9-by-5-in/23-by-12-cm loaf pan with olive oil and dust with tapioca flour.

In a small bowl, whisk 1 Tbsp of the sugar into the warm milk until dissolved. Whisk in the yeast until dissolved. Set aside to proof. The mixture will get foamy. If your kitchen is warm, the mixture will foam quickly—watch it to make sure it doesn't overflow the bowl.

In a medium bowl, mix together the all-purpose flour, xanthan gum, baking powder, salt, and remaining 3 Tbsp sugar. In the bowl of a stand mixer fitted with the paddle attachment, beat the eggs, olive oil, and vinegar on low speed for a few seconds to combine. Add the yeast mixture and beat for a few seconds to combine. Add the flour mixture, beat on low for a few seconds to combine, then increase speed to medium-high and beat for 3 minutes.

Scrape the mixture into the prepared pan and smooth the top. Lightly brush the top with olive oil. Loosely cover with plastic wrap.

Preheat the oven to 375°F/190°C/gas mark 5.

Let the dough stand in a warm, draft-free place to rise until nearly double in bulk, 30 to 40 minutes. (I usually do this on top of the stove while the oven is preheating.) Watch the dough—don't let it rise too much. It should only rise a bit above the top of the pan.

Remove the plastic wrap and bake the bread for 20 minutes. If the top of the bread is getting too brown, tent with aluminum foil. Continue to bake until an instant-read thermometer inserted into the middle reads at least 190°F/88°C, about 10 minutes. Let the bread cool in the pan on a wire rack for 5 minutes, then carefully turn out onto the rack to cool completely.

The bread is best stored at room temperature. I recommend slicing it as needed and then covering the cut side with aluminum foil or setting the cut side down on the cutting board.

¼ cup/60 ml olive oil, plus more for brushing

Tapioca flour for dusting

4 Tbsp/50 g granulated sugar

1½ cups/360 ml warm milk or water (about 110°F/43°C)

2 Tbsp active dry yeast

3 cups/420 g Jeanne's Gluten-Free All-Purpose Flour (page 17)

2 tsp xanthan gum

4 tsp baking powder

1 tsp salt

2 extra-large eggs, at room temperature

2 tsp vinegar, preferably apple cider

DATE NUT BREAD

2 Tbsp unsalted butter, melted and cooled slightly, plus more for greasing

Tapioca flour for dusting

2 cups/280 g Jeanne's Gluten-Free All-Purpose Flour (page 17)

2 tsp baking powder

1 tsp salt

2 extra-large eggs, at room temperature

½ cup/105 g packed brown sugar

½ tsp pure vanilla extract

1 cup/240 ml milk

½ cup/80 g chopped dates

½ cup/60 g chopped pecans

10 SERVINGS When I went to college and started hosting Thanksgiving dinners away from home, I had with me my trusty copy of the *Joy of Cooking*. This is where my mom got all the recipes for our family Thanksgiving feast. It is, therefore, our family recipe treasury. Over the years, I found another recipe from the book that I liked and added it to my Thanksgiving repertoire. I have since adapted it to be gluten-free. In this bread, the sweetness of the dates is tempered by the richness of the pecans, resulting in a slightly sweet and delicate quick bread that is perfect to nibble on before the meal.

Preheat the oven to 350°F/180°C/gas mark 4. Grease a 9-by-5-in/23-by-12-cm loaf pan with melted butter and dust with tapioca flour.

In a medium bowl, mix together the all-purpose flour, baking powder, and salt.

In the bowl of a stand mixer fitted with the paddle attachment, beat the eggs on medium-high speed until light and fluffy, about 2 minutes. Add the brown sugar and beat for 2 minutes. Add the butter and beat until combined. Add the vanilla and beat until combined. Add the flour mixture alternately with the milk in small batches, beginning and ending with the flour mixture. Fold in the dates and nuts. The batter will be stiff.

Scrape batter into the prepared pan and smooth the top. Bake for 45 minutes, or until a toothpick inserted in the middle comes out clean, about 45 minutes. Let sit in the pan for 5 minutes, then unmold onto a wire rack to cool completely.

Store, loosely wrapped in aluminum foil, at room temperature for up to 5 days.

PANETTONE

8 TO 10 SERVINGS There are many theories about the derivation of the name for this traditional Italian holiday bread. According to some, it comes from a person named Toni, and the word is a shortened version of *pan de Toni*, "Toni's bread." Other stories relate that the ingredients were very expensive and that the name is a version of *pan del ton*, "bread of luxury." Whatever the origin, I have always liked this bread. I used to get it at a local Italian grocery each Christmas before I was diagnosed with gluten intolerance. I am thrilled to create this gluten-free version. Like many of its counterparts around the world, panettone is full of dried fruits that have been soaked, or macerated, in alcohol, but it is lighter and sweeter than its German cousin, stollen. Traditionally, the bread is baked in a decorative paper mold that gives it a cylinder shape.

TO MAKE THE MACERATED FRUIT / At least 3 hours before you make the dough, place the raisins and dried fruit in a small bowl. Add the rum and stir to combine. Cover with plastic wrap and let stand at room temperature, stirring every so often. The fruit may also be macerated overnight.

In the bowl of a stand mixer fitted with the paddle attachment, beat the flour, sugar, salt, xanthan gum, baking powder, yeast, lemon zest, and orange zest on low speed for a few seconds to combine. Add the vanilla, whole eggs, and egg yolk and beat for a few more seconds to combine. Add the ½ cup/115 g butter and beat to combine. Add the water and beat to combine, then increase the speed to high and beat for 3 minutes longer.

Grease a large bowl with oil. Scrape the dough into the oiled bowl and loosely cover with plastic wrap. Let stand in a warm, draft-free place to rise until nearly double in bulk, about 2 hours.

Return the dough to the bowl of the stand mixer and fit the mixer with the dough hook. Drain the macerated fruit and discard the liquid. Add the fruit to the dough and beat on low speed for several seconds, until the fruit is well mixed with the dough. You can also do this by hand with a large spoon.

Place a disposable 6-by-4-in/15-by-10-cm paper panettone mold on a cookie sheet. Carefully scrape the dough into the mold. Push the dough around so that it evenly fills the mold, and the mold is round with no points or angles jutting out from the sides. Smooth the top, using a circular motion. Cover very loosely with plastic wrap and let stand in a warm, draft-free place until the dough has risen a bit above the mold, about 1 hour.

Meanwhile, preheat the oven to 375°F/ 190°C/ gas mark 5. (This will give the oven enough time to heat thoroughly.)

Remove the plastic wrap and lightly brush the top of the dough with melted butter. Bake for 30 minutes. Tent the top loosely with

CONTINUED /

MACERATED FRUIT

1 cup/145 g raisins, preferably golden

1 cup/150 g chopped mixed dried fruit, such as apples, apricots, plums, cherries, cranberries, or peaches

½ cup/120 ml rum

3¾ cups/525 g Jeanne's Gluten-Free All-Purpose Flour (page 17)

⅔ cup/130 g granulated sugar

¾ tsp salt

2 tsp xanthan gum

4 tsp baking powder

2 Tbsp active dry yeast

1 tsp grated lemon zest

1 tsp grated orange zest

1 tsp pure vanilla extract

3 extra-large eggs, at room temperature, plus 1 egg yolk, at room temperature

½ cup/115 g unsalted butter, melted and cooled to room temperature, plus melted butter for brushing

1¼ cups/300 ml water, at room temperature

Neutral-tasting oil such as rice bran or canola for greasing

aluminum foil to prevent burning and continue to bake until an instant-read thermometer inserted into the middle of the bread reaches at least 185°F/85°C, about 1 hour. Very carefully place the bread, still in the mold, on a wire rack and let cool completely. Do not slice until it is completely cooled. Serve by ripping the paper away from section you want to slice and then cut into wedges.

Panettone is best within a couple of days after baking. Store at room temperature with the sliced part covered with plastic wrap or aluminum foil for up to 5 days. Microwave or toast slices of the bread to refresh the texture.

STOLLEN

MACERATED FRUIT

1 cup/150 g coarsely chopped mixed dried fruit such as apples, apricots, plums, cherries, cranberries, or peaches

1 cup/145 g golden raisins

½ cup/120 ml brandy

1 Tbsp granulated sugar

1 cup/240 ml warm water (about 110°F/43°C))

2 Tbsp active dry yeast

2¾ cups/385 g Jeanne's Gluten-Free All-Purpose Flour (page 17)

2 tsp xanthan gum

4 tsp baking powder

¾ tsp salt

1 tsp ground cinnamon

1 tsp grated orange zest

1 tsp grated lemon zest

1 extra-large egg, at room temperature

¼ cup/55 g unsalted butter, at room temperature, cut into small pieces

½ cup/120 ml milk

Neutral-flavored oil such as rice bran or canola for brushing

Tapioca flour for dusting

Confectioners' sugar for dusting

10 OR 12 SERVINGS Stollen, a traditional German Christmas yeasted bread made with dried fruit, is similar to Italian panettone. As with many Christmas foods, it has a connection to the baby Jesus and the Three Wise Men. The dough is folded and shaped into a crescent to symbolize a baby's blanket, and the dried fruit symbolizes the gifts from the Wise Men. The bread is traditionally eaten when somewhat dried out, cut into thin slices and served with coffee or tea. My family likes slices of the bread toasted and buttered for breakfast.

TO MAKE THE MACERATED FRUIT / At least 3 hours before you make the dough, place the dried fruit and raisins in a small bowl. Add the brandy and stir to combine. Cover with plastic wrap and let stand at room temperature, stirring every so often. The fruit may also be macerated overnight.

In a small bowl, whisk the granulated sugar into the warm water until dissolved. Whisk in the yeast until dissolved. Set aside to proof. The mixture will get foamy. If your kitchen is warm, the mixture may foam quickly—watch it to make sure it doesn't overflow the bowl.

In the bowl of a stand mixer fitted with the paddle attachment, beat the all-purpose flour, xanthan gum, baking powder, salt, cinnamon, orange zest, and lemon zest on low speed for a few seconds to combine. Add the yeast mixture, egg, butter, and milk and beat briefly to combine. Increase the speed to high and beat for 3 minutes longer.

Brush a large bowl with oil. Scrape the dough into the oiled bowl and loosely cover with plastic wrap. Let stand in a warm, draft-free place to rise until double in bulk, about 2 hours.

Return the dough to the bowl of the stand mixer and fit the mixer with the dough hook. Drain the macerated fruit and discard the liquid. Add the fruit to the dough and beat on low speed until the dough and fruit are combined. You can also do this by hand with a large spoon.

Line a cookie sheet with parchment paper. Liberally dust your rolling surface with tapioca flour. Scrape the dough onto the floured surface and sprinkle with tapioca flour. Roll out the dough to a rough oval or rectangle about ½ in/12 mm thick. It will be about 8 by 10 in/20 by 25 cm. With your hands, gently fold the dough in half. It might break a bit on the underside—just smooth over the break with your fingers. Gently shape the dough into a loose crescent, and squeeze together where the edges of the dough

meet to help seal it. The dough will look kind of messy—that's okay, as it's supposed to look messy. Brush off as much of the tapioca flour as you can with a pastry brush.

Place the dough on the prepared sheet. Cover loosely with plastic wrap and let stand in a warm, draft-free place to rise to about one and a half times its size, about 2 hours.

After 1 hour, preheat the oven to 350°F/180°C/gas mark 4. (This will give the oven enough time to heat thoroughly.)

Remove the plastic wrap and lightly brush the top of the dough with oil. Bake for 20 minutes, then turn the cookie sheet 180 degrees (so the back is now front). Continue to bake until the stollen is a deep brown and an instant-read thermometer inserted into the middle of the bread reaches 190°F/88°C or more, about 50 minutes. Remove the stollen to a wire rack. Immediately brush the top of the stollen with oil and sift confectioners' sugar over the top. Wait for 1 minute and then sift another layer of sugar over the top (there will be a lot of sugar on top). Let cool for at least 1 hour before cutting and serving.

Store in an airtight container for up to 5 days. Microwave or toast slices or pieces of the bread to refresh the texture.

CHEESE CRACKERS AND STRAWS

Cheese crackers and straws are terrific party snacks, especially for New Year's Eve. They are simple to prepare and get rave reviews from guests. Sometimes I make them with cheese only, and sometimes I add a pinch of cayenne for a little kick. You can also experiment with your own choice of herbs and spices. The recipe here calls for both Cheddar cheese and Parmesan. If you like, you can use Cheddar alone, by replacing the Parmesan with the same amount of Cheddar.

1½ cups/210 g Jeanne's Gluten-Free All-Purpose Flour (page 17)

¼ tsp salt

⅛ tsp cayenne pepper (optional)

½ tsp dried herb such as thyme or rosemary or ground spice such as cumin (optional)

6 Tbsp/85 g cold unsalted butter, cut into pieces

2½ cups/175 g grated Cheddar cheese

1 cup/70 g grated Parmesan cheese

1 extra-large egg

¼ cup/60 ml milk

Preheat the oven to 400°F/200°C/gas mark 5. Line two baking sheets with parchment paper.

In a food processor, combine the flour, salt, cayenne (if using), and dried herb (if using). Pulse a few times to mix. Add the butter and both the cheeses and pulse until evenly mixed with the dry ingredients, about 1 minute. The dough will look like wet sand with pebbles. Add the egg and pulse until incorporated. With the motor running, pour the milk through the feed tube and blend until the dough forms a ball. (Alternatively, you may mix the dough by hand, using a pastry cutter to combine the dry ingredients and the butter and cheeses. Then, with a wooden spoon, stir in the egg and milk. The dough will be very stiff.) Divide the dough into two equal portions.

TO MAKE CRACKER ROUNDS / Place a portion of the dough between two pieces of waxed paper and roll to ⅛ in/3 mm thick. Using a 2-in/5-cm cookie cutter, cut out as many rounds as possible. Using a spatula, place the cutouts on a prepared sheet, spacing them at least ½ in/12 mm apart. Roll out the dough scraps and repeat the process until all the dough is used.

TO MAKE STRAWS / From a portion of dough, pinch off a marble-sized piece of dough. Roll into a ball and then put on a piece of waxed paper and roll into an evenly shaped cylinder about 5½ in/14 cm long. Place on a prepared sheet. Repeat until all the dough is used, spacing the cylinders at least ½ in/12 mm apart.

Place the sheets on the middle and lower oven racks. Bake until the crackers or straws are brownish around the edges, 15 to 20 minutes. They will be moderately crunchy. Let the crackers or straws cool on the cookie sheets until you can pick them up, then remove to wire racks to cool completely.

Store in an airtight container at room temperature for up to 5 days.

STUFFING LIKE MAMA MADE

ABOUT 7 CUPS/1.6 L

This stuffing is similar to the one my mother prepared every Thanksgiving while we were growing up. We loved it. No matter what else had leftovers, the stuffing was always gone by the end of the meal. After I moved out and started hosting my own Thanksgiving dinners, I continued to use her recipe. The beauty of the recipe is that it is made with simple, easy-to-find ingredients. Each adds just the right note to the whole symphony of flavors and textures. The bread base provides the soft texture. The nuts and celery give it crunch. The shallots and onion provide the savory undertones that work with the mushrooms, and the tarragon adds a delicate, not-too-strong anise flavor that plays off of the nutmeg and pulls everything together. This recipe provides enough to stuff a good-sized turkey, but the instructions are for baking on its own. If any vegans are sharing your table, the stuffing can be made without animal products.

For safety's sake, be sure to stuff the turkey loosely and to have both the turkey and the stuffing at room temperature—cold stuffing should not go into the turkey.

4 Tbsp/55 g unsalted butter or olive oil

¼ cup/30 g minced shallots

1 cup/95 g sliced white button mushrooms

¼ cup/35 g chopped yellow onion

1 cup/115 g chopped celery

4 cups/320 g slightly toasted bread cubes from Sandwich Bread (page 125)

1 tsp dried tarragon

Salt

½ tsp paprika

⅛ tsp freshly grated nutmeg

¼ to ½ cup/60 to 120 ml chicken or vegetable stock

1½ cups/180 g chopped pecans

Freshly ground pepper

Preheat the oven to 350°F/180°C/gas mark 4. In a large frying pan or sauté pan over medium heat, melt 2 Tbsp of the butter. Add the shallots and sauté for 2 minutes. Add the mushrooms and sauté until soft, about 5 minutes. Scrape into a bowl and put aside.

Add the remaining 2 Tbsp butter to the pan over medium heat. Add the onion and celery and sauté until soft, about 5 minutes. Remove from the heat, add the bread cubes, and toss until the bread is combined with the vegetables. Add the tarragon, 1 tsp salt, paprika, and nutmeg and toss to combine. Stir in enough stock to moisten the mixture slightly. Add the pecans and the mushroom mixture and toss to combine. Season with salt and pepper. Put the stuffing in a 8-in/20-cm square baking pan and bake until the stuffing is light brown on top, about 30 minutes. Serve immediately.

06 DEEP-FRIED TREATS

COOKING DOUGH IN HOT OIL DATES BACK TO ANCIENT TIMES. And, it is a practice found in cultures around the world. In writings from the second century BCE, Cato the Elder mentioned frying *scribilita* ("pastry") in oil. Chinese Buddhist monks have fried sweet cakes for holy days for hundreds of years. Medieval European "cryspeys" were made with a batter that was allowed to stream down the maker's fingers into the oil, creating something like our modern funnel cakes. Dutch settlers in the United States are credited with introducing what we now know as doughnuts, called *oly koekes* ("oily cakes") in the early nineteenth century.

Because oil has been quite expensive for most of history, it is traditional to find oil-fried foods saved for special times of the year—particularly holiday periods. During the Jewish celebration of Hanukkah, fried *sufganiyot* ("jelly doughnuts"), are enjoyed. Latin American cultures have fried tortillas called *buñuelos* for Christmas, while Norwegians have delicate rosettes. Italians make *struffoli* (fried dough balls) and *cannoli* (fried and stuffed dough tubes) for the Christmas season. In our own family here in the United States, we like to make pumpkin doughnuts during the fall and winter festive season. Regardless of the culture they are from, these treats offer delectable ways to enjoy a bit of fried indulgence during this special time of year.

PUMPKIN DOUGHNUTS

ABOUT 30 DOUGHNUTS AND DOUGHNUT HOLES

These doughnuts are a favorite whenever I serve them. I discovered them when my daughter began elementary school. Her teacher had a tradition of offering pumpkin doughnuts to the parents who attended the autumn open house. And, as soon as I adapted them to be gluten-free, I discovered why. They are a worthy addition to the traditions of fall. The spices are subtle enough to allow the pumpkin flavor to shine through, and the lightly crunchy exterior gives way to the soft, pumpkiny interior. To me, they taste like the comfort of being indoors, cuddling with my daughter, on a cold, blustery day. Dipping them in a cinnamon-sugar coating takes them to the next level.

4 cups/560 g Jeanne's Gluten-Free All-Purpose Flour (page 17)

2 tsp salt

4 tsp baking powder

½ tsp baking soda

1 tsp freshly grated nutmeg

½ tsp ground cinnamon, plus 2 Tbsp

¼ tsp ground ginger

2 extra-large eggs, at room temperature

1½ cups/300 g granulated sugar

2 Tbsp neutral-flavored oil such as rice bran or canola, plus more for frying

1 cup/240 ml canned pumpkin purée

½ cup/120 ml buttermilk

Tapioca flour for dusting

In a medium bowl, mix together the flour, salt, baking powder, baking soda, nutmeg, ½ tsp cinnamon, and ginger.

In the bowl of a stand mixer fitted with the paddle attachment, beat the eggs and 1 cup/200 g sugar on medium-high speed until light and fluffy, about 2 minutes. Add the 2 Tbsp oil and beat until combined. Add the pumpkin purée and beat until combined. Add the flour mixture alternately with the buttermilk in small batches, beginning and ending with the flour. Beat until just combined. Divide the dough into three equal portions. Shape each into a disk (the disks will be quite soft) and wrap tightly in plastic wrap. Refrigerate the dough until it has firmed up a bit, 1 to 2 hours.

Pour 3 to 4 in/7.5 to 10 cm of oil into a deep, heavy-bottomed 2-qt/2-L saucepan. Heat over medium-high heat until the oil reaches 360°F/182°C on a candy thermometer.

While the oil is heating, remove a dough disk from the refrigerator and place between two pieces of waxed paper. Roll to about ¾ in/2 cm thick (no thinner). Have ready a cookie sheet to hold the cut doughnuts. Using a doughnut cutter dipped in tapioca flour, cut out as many doughnuts as you can. You can also use two round cookie cutters, a large one about 2½ in/6.5 cm to cut out the doughnuts and a small one about 1 in/2.5 cm to cut out the doughnut holes. Place the cutout doughnuts on the cookie sheet. Gather and roll out the scraps, then cut out more doughnuts and holes.

Have ready a platter lined with paper towels. Using a spatula, carefully lower the doughnuts and doughnut holes into the hot oil. Cook only as many doughnuts as will fit comfortably in your pan, allowing some space between them so that they can fry all the way around. As you place the doughnuts in the oil, the oil will start to foam—this means that the doughnuts are cooking. When the doughnuts rise to the surface, after about 30 seconds, carefully turn them with tongs. Fry until the doughnuts are golden brown, about 3 minutes total, turning them every 30 seconds. With the tongs, remove the doughnuts from the oil and place on the paper towels to drain. Allow the oil to return to 360°F/182°C, and repeat until all the doughnuts are fried. Be sure to monitor the oil so that the temperature remains constant; you may need to adjust the heat as you fry each batch. You don't want the temperature to rise above 365°F/185°C, because the doughnuts will burn before they are cooked through.

Repeat the rolling, cutting, and frying process with the remaining dough disks.

In a small bowl, stir together the 2 Tbsp cinnamon and ½ cup/100 g sugar. Place one side or both sides of each doughnut in the cinnamon-sugar, and then arrange the coated doughnuts on a serving plate.

Store in an airtight container at room temperature for up to 5 days.

SUFGANIYOT
(JELLY DOUGHNUTS)

ABOUT 20 DOUGHNUTS

The eight days of Hanukkah, the Jewish celebration of lights, honor the sacred lamp in the Holy Temple, which burned for eight days even though it only contained enough oil for one. Traditionally, many Hanukkah foods celebrate the oil in addition to the light. One of the most common is the jelly doughnut, known as *sufganiyah*. The word derives from the Hebrew word for "sponge," an apt description for the texture of the doughnuts. I think they are more accurately "pillowy."

1 tsp granulated sugar, plus
¾ cup/150 g

¾ cup plus 2 Tbsp/210 ml warm water (about 110°F/43°C)

1 Tbsp active dry yeast

2 cups/280 g Jeanne's Gluten-Free All-Purpose Flour (page 17)

1 tsp salt

1 tsp xanthan gum

2 tsp baking powder

1 extra-large egg, at room temperature

1 Tbsp unsalted butter, melted and cooled a bit

Neutral-flavored oil such as rice bran or canola for greasing and frying

Tapioca flour for dusting

¼ cup/60 ml jam of your choice such as raspberry

In a small bowl, whisk the 1 tsp sugar into the warm water until dissolved. Whisk in the yeast until dissolved. Set aside to proof. The mixture will get foamy. If your kitchen is warm, the mixture may foam quickly—watch it to make sure it doesn't overflow the bowl.

In a medium bowl, mix together the all-purpose flour, salt, xanthan gum, baking powder, and ¼ cup/50 g of the sugar.

In the bowl of a stand mixer fitted with the paddle attachment, beat the egg, butter, and yeast mixture on low speed for a few seconds to combine. Add the flour mixture and beat for a few seconds to combine. Increase the speed to high and beat for 3 minutes longer.

Grease a large bowl with oil. Scrape the dough into the oiled bowl and cover with plastic wrap. Let the dough stand in a warm, draft-free place until nearly double in bulk, about 1 hour.

Liberally dust your rolling surface with tapioca flour. Line two cookie sheets with waxed paper. These will be your holding trays for the cut dough. Place the dough on the floured surface and dust with tapioca flour.

Gently roll the dough to about ⅛ in/6 mm thick. With a 2¼-in/5.75-cm cookie cutter, cut out as many rounds as possible, dipping the cutter into tapioca flour before each cut. With a spatula dipped in tapioca flour, scoop up the rounds and place on the prepared sheets, spacing them at least 1 in/2.5 cm apart. Flour your hands with tapioca flour, gather the remaining dough, and squish it a few times to smooth it out, then repeat the process until all the dough is used. Try to do this in as few batches as you can. It's fine if some of the last cut rounds have some folds. You should aim for 40 rounds (you need an even amount).

Using a pastry brush, brush off as much tapioca flour as you can from the cut rounds. Place ¼ tsp jam in the center of half of the rounds. With a finger dipped in water, moisten the dough around the jam. Set a plain round on top of each jam-covered round. Press around the edges to seal, then push the edges toward the center so each doughnut is fat and fluffy. You may also want to bring the cookie cutter down around the perimeter of each doughnut

CONTINUED /

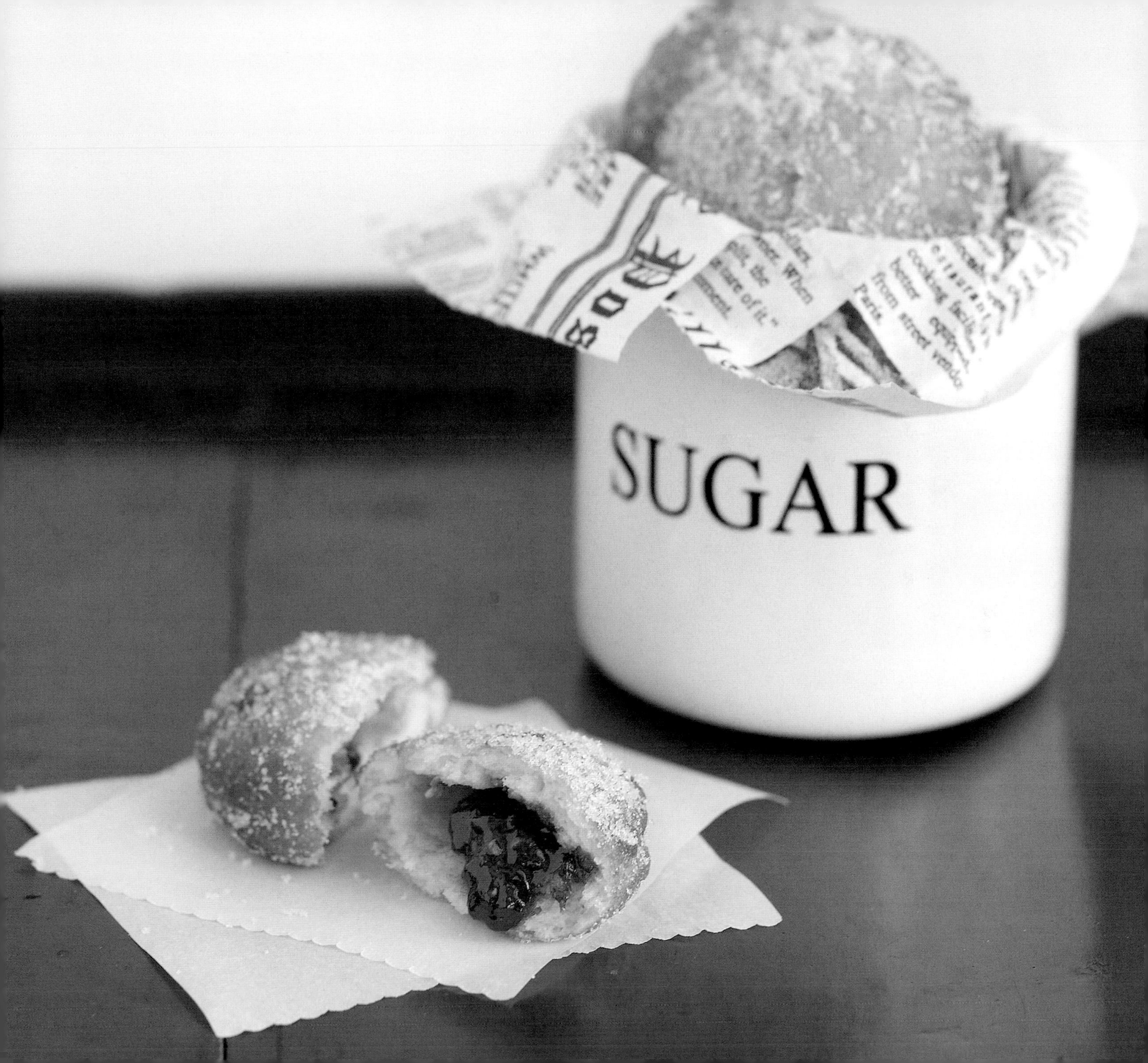
SUGAR

to cut off any extra dough sticking out from the circle and to further seal the sides. Let the doughnuts stand in a warm, draft-free place until they are puffy and about double in bulk, about 1 hour.

About 30 minutes before the doughnuts have risen fully, pour 3 to 4 in/7.5 to 10 cm of oil into a deep, heavy-bottomed 2-qt/2-L saucepan. Heat over medium-high heat until the oil reaches 375°F/190°C on a candy thermometer. Have ready one or two platters lined with paper towels.

Using the spatula, carefully lower the doughnuts into the hot oil. Cook only as many doughnuts as will fit comfortably in your pan, allowing some space between them so that they can fry all the way around. As you place the doughnuts in the oil, the oil will start to foam—this means that the doughnuts are cooking. Fry the doughnuts until brown on one side, about 40 seconds, then turn and fry until the doughnuts are brown on the second side,

and puffed and golden, about 20 seconds. With tongs, remove the doughnuts from the oil and place on the paper towels to drain. Allow the oil to return to 375°F/190°C, and repeat until all the doughnuts are fried. Be sure to monitor the oil so that the temperature remains constant; you may need to adjust the heat as you fry each batch. You don't want the oil to go above 380°F/193°C, because the doughnuts will burn before they are cooked through.

Set a wire rack over a cookie sheet. Place the remaining ½ cup/100 g sugar in a bowl. Gently roll each warm doughnut in the sugar until coated. Set on the rack to cool completely.

Doughnuts made with yeasted dough are best eaten the day they are fried. Only make as many as you plan to eat that day. The dough may be stored in the refrigerator for up to 2 days.

PIZZELLES

4 DOZEN COOKIES — *Pizzelles* are traditional Italian waffle cookies often made around the holidays. The word *pizze* means "round and flat" and is also the base of the word *pizza*. True to their name, *pizzelles* are flat, round cookies. They are made in a specialized *pizzelle* iron that imprints a festive design on the cookies (see pages 26–27). You can make flat cookies or roll them around a small dowel that usually comes with the iron to make small tubes. The cookies are simple, crunchy, and addictive. Because this recipe makes so many, it's terrific for parties—the cookies are very pretty when presented on a large plate. I give you three flavorings to choose from. The traditional Italian flavoring is anise, but I also like vanilla or lemon. Here, the cookies are dusted with confectioners' sugar. I also like to eat them as elegant ice-cream sandwiches, with a dollop of ice cream in the middle.

3 extra-large eggs, at room temperature

1 cup/200 g granulated sugar

½ cup/115 g unsalted butter, melted and cooled slightly

1 Tbsp crushed anise seeds, or 1 tsp pure vanilla extract, or 1 tsp grated lemon zest

2 cups/280 g Jeanne's Gluten-Free All-Purpose Flour (page 17)

½ tsp ground cinnamon

Neutral-flavored oil such as rice bran or canola for brushing

Confectioners' sugar for dusting

In a large bowl, whisk the eggs until foamy, about 1 minute. Add the granulated sugar and whisk until combined and foamy, about 1 minute. Continuing to whisk, slowly add the butter and whisk until combined. Add the anise seeds and whisk until combined. Add the flour and cinnamon and whisk until combined. The batter will be thick.

Cover the bowl and refrigerate for 30 minutes to allow the flavors to meld and the batter to thicken. The batter will reach a thick consistency almost like cookie dough.

Preheat the *pizzelle* iron to the temperature recommended in the manufacturer's instructions. I set mine to 3.5. Brush the inside with oil. Most irons only need to be oiled for the first use. After that, the iron should be fairly nonstick. Have ready a cookie sheet to hold the cooked *pizzelles* while they cool. Spoon the batter in the amount recommended for your

iron into the middle of each section and then slowly close and lock the lid. My iron makes 3-in/7.5-cm cookies, so I use a heaping 1 tsp for each. Cook for 1 minute, or according to the instructions. Open the lid and use tongs to remove the cookies. They should be a mottled light brown or cream color. Set on the cookie sheet to cool flat. The cookies will crisp as they cool. Once the cookies have cooled a bit, you can stack them to make more room on the sheet. It may take a few batches to get the hang of centering the cookies on the iron. Also, if the batter goes over the design, you can trim the *pizzelles* with kitchen shears after they cool.

Before serving, dust confectioners' sugar over each cookie. Only put sugar on as many cookies as you are going to eat that day.

Store in an airtight container at room temperature for up to 2 weeks. Dust the cookies with sugar as you serve them.

KRUMKAKE

20 COOKIES These delicate waffle-cone cookies are a traditional Norwegian Christmas treat. They are made by cooking a simple batter on a special waffle iron inscribed with a scroll-like pattern (pages 26–27). *Krumkake* means "curved cake" in Norwegian. The cookies are rolled into a cone shape with a cone roller and then filled. The filling is customarily whipped cream sweetened with jam, often made from cloudberries. You can also use the jam of your choice. Don't be intimidated by the cooking and rolling process—*krumkake* are quite easy to make, and the process is addicting. Once I get started, it's hard for me to stop. They are fun to make with kids. *Krumkake* are somewhat like a very delicate ice cream cone—crisp and lightly sweet, tasting of vanilla.

1 cup/200 g granulated sugar

½ cup/115 g unsalted butter, at room temperature

1 tsp pure vanilla extract

2 extra-large eggs, at room temperature

1½ cups/210 g Jeanne's Gluten-Free All-Purpose Flour (page 17)

1 cup/240 ml milk

Neutral-flavored oil such as rice bran or canola for brushing

2 cups/480 ml heavy cream, chilled

½ cup/120 ml cloudberry jam or other jam of your choice

In the bowl of a stand mixer fitted with the paddle attachment, beat the sugar and butter until fluffy, about 3 minutes. Add the vanilla and beat until blended. Add the eggs, one at a time, and beat until the mixture is light and fluffy, about 1 minute. Add the flour alternately with the milk in small batches, beginning and ending with the flour. Beat until the batter is smooth, a few seconds.

Preheat the *krumkake* iron to the temperature recommended in the manufacturer's instructions. If you have an electric iron, preheat it to the 2.5 darkness level. Brush the iron with a bit of oil. You will probably only need to brush the iron with oil for the first cookie, but see how your iron behaves and brush accordingly. Spoon 1 Tbsp of the batter in the middle of the iron and close the top. Cook until the cookie is firm and slightly brown, 60 to 70 seconds. You will need to make a few cookies to determine the optimal cooking time for your iron. Using tongs, remove the cookie from the iron to a plate or cookie sheet and quickly roll it around the roller cone with your hands (it will be hot), pressing lightly on the edge to seal. Let stand until the cookie has cooled into the cone shape, 1 to 2 minutes. Remove the cookie from the roller cone, let it cool for another minute, then transfer to a different plate to cool completely. The cookies will crisp as they cool. Repeat the process with the remaining batter.

Just before serving, place the cream in the bowl of a stand mixer fitted with the whisk attachment. Beat until the cream forms just barely stiff peaks. (Don't whip it too long because it will turn into butter.) Stir in the jam. Spoon the cream into the cookies, filling them three-fourths full.

The cookies can be made ahead and stored, unfilled, in an airtight container at room temperature for up to 1 week. Don't fill the cookies until you are ready to serve them; cookies filled in advance will become soggy.

ROSETTES

3 DOZEN ROSETTES Rosettes are deep-fried, very fragile Christmas cookies of Norwegian origin. They are somewhat like a delicate funnel cake. The name comes from the original and most popular shape in which they are made. When I was in middle school, I took a cooking class that confirmed forever my passion for cooking and baking. The teacher, a big woman named Mrs. Baker, was somewhat cranky, but I adored her and couldn't wait to get to class each day. Every week, the class divided into small groups and prepared a meal using the ingredients and techniques that she had taught us. One week we learned how to make rosettes. It wasn't until I was an adult that I realized that not everyone knew how to make rosettes or even what they are. They are deceptively easy and pretty to look at. You will need a rosette iron to make these (see page 27).

1 cup/140 g Jeanne's Gluten-Free All-Purpose Flour (page 17)

¼ tsp salt

2 extra-large eggs, at room temperature

2 tsp pure vanilla extract

1 cup/240 ml milk

Neutral-flavored oil such as rice bran or canola for frying

Confectioners' sugar for dusting

In a small bowl, mix together the flour and salt. In a medium bowl, whisk together the eggs, vanilla, and milk. Add the flour mixture and whisk until the batter is somewhat thick, about the texture of heavy cream or pancake batter. Cover and refrigerate for 2 hours. This is not absolutely necessary, but will help yield crunchy rosettes.

Pour 3 to 4 in/7.5 to 10 cm of oil into a deep, heavy-bottomed 2-qt/2-L saucepan. If using irons made of cast iron, heat the oil to 350°F/177°C and keep the cooking temperature in the 350° to 365°F/177° to 185°C range. If using irons made of cast aluminum, heat the oil to 325°F/163°C and keep the cooking temperature in the 325° to 335°F/163° to 170°C range.

Screw the rosette iron you want to use onto the iron's handle. Pour some of the batter into a flat-bottomed glass, pottery, or metal container—don't use plastic or another material that will melt from the heat of the hot rosette iron. This will be your working batter. Return the remaining batter to the refrigerator. Have ready a large plate lined with paper towels.

Carefully submerge the iron in the hot oil for 10 to 20 seconds (20 seconds for the first few rosettes, then 10 seconds after you've used the iron a few times). Lift the iron from the oil and dip it into the batter, being careful to cover the bottom and sides of the iron but not the top. Quickly lift the iron from the batter and submerge it in the hot oil, making sure it is completely covered with oil but does not touch the bottom of the pan. The oil will bubble and foam quite a bit. Fry the rosette until light brown, 25 to 40 seconds. Lift the iron from the oil. With a fork or butter knife, carefully remove the rosette from the iron to the paper towels to drain. Every so often a rosette may come off the iron while it's in the oil. That's okay—just let it fry until light brown and then remove it from the oil with a fork and let drain.

CONTINUED /

Repeat the process with the remaining batter in the container. As you get low on working batter, add more chilled batter. You will notice that the working batter will become warm and will stop attaching to the rosette iron. As this happens, replenish with cold batter.

When the rosettes have cooled, place on a clean plate and dust confectioners' sugar over the top.

Store in an airtight container at room temperature for up to 5 days.

NOTE: *If you have new rosette irons that have never been used, you need to season them. Put the irons in a saucepan and fill with 3 to 4 in/7.5 to 10 cm of oil. Heat over medium-high heat until the oil reaches 350° to 365°F/177° to 185°C on a candy thermometer. Let the irons sit in the hot oil for 20 minutes. Watch the thermometer and keep the oil within the given range. Remove the irons from the oil with tongs and drain on a cookie sheet lined with paper towels. You can use the same oil for frying the rosettes.*

STRUFFOLI

These traditional Christmas pastries from Naples, Italy, are marble-size balls of fried dough covered with a honey glaze that is meant to symbolize the wish for a sweet year ahead. They are basically doughnuts, with a crispy exterior that yields to a soft, pillowy interior. *Struffoli* comes from a word meaning "rounded." The Neapolitan treats are piled attractively on a plate and then decorated festively with sprinkles. Some families like to give away plates of *struffoli*. If you want to do this, cover the bottom of four small paper plates with aluminum foil. Place equal mounds of *struffoli* on each and drizzle with any leftover glaze. Decorate with sprinkles, if you like, and let set for about 2 hours.

2 cups/280 g Jeanne's Gluten-Free All-Purpose Flour (page 17)

1 tsp grated lemon zest

1 tsp grated orange or tangerine zest

3 Tbsp granulated sugar

½ tsp salt

¾ tsp baking powder

¼ cup/55 g cold unsalted butter, cut into 8 pieces

3 extra-large eggs, at room temperature

1 tsp pure vanilla extract

1 Tbsp marsala, white wine, or water

Neutral-flavored oil such as rice bran or canola for frying

Tapioca flour for dusting

HONEY GLAZE

¼ cup/60 ml honey

¼ cup/50 g granulated sugar

1 Tbsp grated orange or lemon zest

Gluten-free sprinkles for decorating (optional)

In the bowl of a stand mixer fitted with the paddle attachment, beat the flour, lemon zest, orange zest, sugar, salt, and baking powder on low speed for a few seconds until combined. Increase the speed to medium, add the butter, and beat until the mixture looks like a combination of flakes, gravel, and flour, about 2 minutes. Add the eggs, vanilla, and marsala and beat until the dough comes together in a cohesive mass. Shape the dough into a disk, wrap tightly in plastic wrap, and refrigerate for 1 hour to firm up a bit.

Pour 3 to 4 in/7.5 to 10 cm of oil into a deep, heavy-bottomed 2-qt/2-L saucepan. Heat over medium-high heat until the oil reaches 350°F/177°C on a candy thermometer.

While the oil is heating, remove the dough disk from the refrigerator and divide into four fairly equal pieces. Rewrap three of the pieces and return to the refrigerator. Dust your rolling surface with tapioca flour. You want to work quickly so the dough doesn't warm up too much. If it does and becomes too floppy to work with, return the dough to the refrigerator to firm up. With your hands, roll the dough into a rope about ½ in/12 mm thick. Cut the rope crosswise into roughly ½-in/12-mm pieces. Roll each piece between your hands into a ball about the size of a marble. Place the balls on a platter. Repeat with the remaining pieces of dough. You will have about 120 balls of dough.

Have ready a cookie sheet lined with paper towels. Fill a slotted spoon with dough balls and carefully lower them into the hot oil. I touch the spoon to the oil, then tip the balls into the oil. This helps keep me from getting splashed with hot oil. Cook only as many balls as will fit comfortably in your pan, allowing some space between them. Fry until the balls are a light golden brown, 2 to 2½ minutes. With a large spoon, carefully move the balls around in the oil every so often so that they fry evenly. I find that they often clump on one side of the pan. Remove the balls from the oil with the

CONTINUED /

slotted spoon and place on the paper towels to drain. Repeat the process to fry the remaining balls. Allow the oil to return to 350°F/177°C between each batch. Be sure to monitor the oil so that the temperature remains constant but does not exceed 365°F/185°C.

TO MAKE THE HONEY GLAZE / In a large heavy-bottomed saucepan, combine the honey, sugar, and orange zest. Cook over medium heat, stirring often, until the sugar is dissolved, about 4 minutes. Remove from the heat.

Carefully place all the *struffoli* in the saucepan with the glaze and stir with a large spoon until the balls are covered. Let sit in the pan while you ready a serving plate.

The *struffoli* can be shaped into a wreath or stacked into a pyramid shape. For a wreath, rub a straight-sided glass with oil and place in the center of a large plate. Spoon the *struffoli* around the glass. Drizzle with any leftover glaze. Decorate with sprinkles (if desired). Allow to set for 2 hours and then remove the glass. For a pyramid, with a spoon or damp hands, place layers of *struffoli* on top of each other on a plate, gently shaping them into a pyramid or cone. Drizzle with any leftover glaze. Decorate with sprinkles (if using). Allow to set for at least 2 hours.

Store in an airtight container at room temperature for up to 5 days.

BUÑUELOS

Of the several versions of these Latin American treats, the one I know the best is the Mexican *buñuelo*, a deep-fried tortilla sprinkled with a cinnamon-sugar coating. The *buñuelos* are eaten during Las Posadas, a celebration reenacting Mary and Joseph's journey from Nazareth to Bethlehem in their search for an inn. I grew up in Monterey, California, which has a strong connection with Mexican culture. I remember a celebration one evening when actors playing Mary and Joseph, along with kids and adults as shepherds, walked the streets, stopping at the historic adobe houses to sing a request for shelter. Stationed at each adobe were other actors playing innkeepers, who sang back that there was no room. We ended up at an adobe with a small barn for animals and an innkeeper who sang a welcome song. Everyone, both actors and spectators, enjoyed a huge party to celebrate the season. It is still a special memory for me!

1½ cups/360 ml water, at room temperature

1 extra-large egg, at room temperature

3 Tbsp granulated sugar, plus ½ cup/100 g

3 Tbsp unsalted butter, melted and cooled

1 Tbsp rum, brandy, or water

½ tsp salt

5 cups/700 g Jeanne's Gluten-Free All-Purpose Flour (page 17)

1 Tbsp ground cinnamon

Neutral-flavored oil such as rice bran or canola for frying

Tapioca flour for dusting

In a large bowl, whisk together the water, egg, 3 Tbsp sugar, butter, rum, and salt. Add 4 cups/ 560 g of the flour, 1 cup/140 g at a time, stirring with a large spoon after each addition. The dough should be quite stiff. Sprinkle some of the remaining flour on your rolling surface. Turn out the dough onto the floured surface. Sprinkle the dough with small batches of the flour, kneading and turning the dough after each addition. After all the flour has been incorporated, knead and turn dough until it is smooth. Shape into a nicely rounded ball, return to the bowl, cover with plastic wrap, and let rest at room temperature for 1 hour.

While the dough rests, combine the ½ cup/ 100 g sugar with the cinnamon in a small bowl. Stir to combine and put aside.

Pour 3 to 4 in/7.5 to 10 cm of oil into a deep, heavy-bottomed 2-qt/2-L saucepan. Heat over medium-high heat until the oil reaches 350°F/177°C on a candy thermometer.

Dust your rolling surface with tapioca flour. Pull off a 1-Tbsp piece of dough and roll into a ball with your hands. Set on the floured surface. With a rolling pin, roll the ball once, then turn the dough a bit, and roll again. You want to roll out a round that is as thin as possible. Repeat the rolling and turning until the round is about 6 in/15 cm in diameter and quite thin. The thinner the dough, the more crunchy the *buñuelo* will be. If you watch a Mexican grandmother form the dough, you will see that she pulls the dough. Gluten-free dough isn't pliable enough to do this, so it needs to be rolled. Place the rounds on a cookie sheet to dry a bit. Stack the dough rounds with pieces of parchment paper between the layers.

Have ready three plates each lined with a few layers of paper towels. Carefully slip a dough round into the hot oil. The *buñuelo* should start to develop air bubbles on the surface. Cook for about 1 minute and then

carefully turn the round with tongs. The second side will develop air bubbles. Continue to fry until the *buñuelo* is light brown on both sides, about 1½ minutes. With the tongs, lift the *buñuelo* from the oil and allow the excess oil to drip into the saucepan. Place the *buñuelo* on a lined plate and sprinkle with a large pinch of the cinnamon-sugar—the top should be nicely covered.

Allow the oil to return to 350°F/177°C and repeat the process to fry the remaining dough rounds. Be sure to monitor the oil and adjust the heat if necessary so that the temperature remains constant. As you fry the remaining rounds, place each *buñuelo* on top of the previously cooked *buñuelo*. After cooking about 10 *buñuelos*, start stacking them on the second plate. Repeat with the third plate, which will contain 12 *buñuelos*.

Store in an airtight container at room temperature for up to 5 days.

CANNOLI

ABOUT 20 CANNOLI *Cannoli* are Sicilian treats originally eaten during the Mardi Gras season. Nowadays, they are enjoyed year-round, but because of their association with festivals, they have a particular connection to the Christmas season. *Cannolo*, the singular form, means "little tube." This word, in turn, comes from the Latin for "reed." Originally, a tube made out of a reed helped the cannoli keep their shape while being fried. Now, the tubes are metal. The pastries are stuffed with a sweetened ricotta filling. It's easy to understand why cannoli are so beloved: they have a crisp cookie shell and are filled with a creamy, sweet filling punctuated by chocolate chips.

TO MAKE THE CANNOLI SHELLS / In a medium bowl, mix together the flour, salt, cinnamon, and granulated sugar. With a pastry cutter or your fingers, cut or squish the butter pieces into the dry ingredients until the mixture resembles sand with pebbles. Add the whole egg and mix with a fork until completely combined. Add the marsala and use your hands to combine. The dough should come together but not quite hold together. Add the water, 1 Tbsp at a time, until the dough just holds together. You may not need all the water or you may need more—the humidity of your kitchen will determine the amount. Knead the dough in the bowl for 1 minute to make it smooth and ensure that everything is evenly distributed.

Shape the dough into a disk, wrap tightly in plastic wrap and refrigerate for 1 hour. This will allow the liquid to distribute throughout the dough, as well as let the dough firm up a bit.

Dust your rolling surface with tapioca flour. Remove the dough from the refrigerator. Place it on the floured surface and dust with tapioca flour. Roll out to ⅛ in/3 mm thick (any thicker and the fried dough doesn't crisp up as much as it should; any thinner and it starts to tear when you try to wrap it around the cannoli tubes). Using a 3½-in/9-cm cookie cutter, cut out as many rounds as you can. Place the rounds on a small plate, one on top of the other. Roll out the scraps and cut more dough rounds. Cover the stack of dough rounds with plastic wrap so they don't dry out.

Pour 3 to 4 in/7.5 to 10 cm of oil into a deep, heavy-bottomed 2-qt/2-L saucepan. Heat over medium-high heat until the oil reaches 325°F/160°C on a candy thermometer.

Working with one dough round at a time, brush off the tapioca flour with a pastry brush. Put the round on another plate—this will be your working plate. Place a metal cannoli tube in the middle of the dough round. Bring one side of the dough round up and over the tube, then bring the other side up and over the tube. Dip a finger in the egg wash and use it to seal the edges, pressing them together

CONTINUED /

CANNOLI SHELLS

1½ cups/210 g Jeanne's Gluten-Free All-Purpose Flour (page 17)

¼ tsp salt

¼ tsp ground cinnamon

¼ cup/50 g granulated sugar

¼ cup/55 g cold unsalted butter, cut into small pieces

1 extra-large egg; plus 1 extra-large egg beaten with 1 Tbsp water, for egg wash

2 Tbsp cold marsala or white wine

2 to 3 Tbsp cold water

Tapioca flour for dusting

Neutral-flavored oil such as rice bran or canola for frying

FILLING

About 1 lb/455 g fresh sheep's or cow's milk ricotta cheese, drained (see note)

½ cup/100 g granulated sugar

3 Tbsp grated orange zest

⅓ cup/60 g mini semisweet chocolate chips

¼ tsp ground cinnamon (optional)

Confectioners' sugar for dusting (optional)

Mini semisweet chocolate chips for decorating (optional)

gently. You will want to feather the top edge over the bottom edge a bit to make sure that the edges are firmly sealed. If they aren't, the tubes of dough will unwrap in the hot oil.

Have ready a cookie sheet lined with two layers of paper towels for draining the cannoli shells. Line a large plate with paper towels. Using tongs, carefully lower the dough-wrapped cannoli tubes into the hot oil. As you place the tubes in the oil, the oil will start to foam—this means that the dough is cooking. Cook only as many tubes as will fit comfortably in your pan, allowing some space between them so that they can fry all the way around. Fry, turning the tubes a few times so they don't burn on the bottom, until they are golden brown, about 3 minutes. Using the tongs, remove the tubes to the lined cooking sheet to drain. Be sure to monitor the oil so that the temperature remains between 320°F/160°C and 325°F/163°C.

When the tubes have cooled enough that they can be handled but are still hot, gently remove the shells from the tubes and place on the lined plate to cool completely. If a shell sticks to the metal tube, place a layer or two of paper towels on the counter, then hit the end of the metal tube on the lined counter while holding the cooked shell. This should dislodge the shell. Be sure that you hold the shell, not the metal under the shell, which is hotter than the exposed metal.

Let the metal tubes stand until they are cool to the touch. Repeat the process until all the dough rounds are fried. Allow the oil to return to 325°F/163°C between batches.

TO MAKE THE FILLING / Place the drained ricotta in a medium bowl. Discard the liquid. Add the granulated sugar, orange zest, chocolate chips, and cinnamon (if using) and stir until combined.

Spoon the filling into a pastry bag fitted with a wide round tip. Pipe the filling into one end of each shell, then turn the shell and pipe the filling into the other end. Dust confectioners' sugar (if using) over each cannoli. Dip the ends of the cannoli into a bowl of mini chocolate chips (if using). The cannoli should be served soon after filling, or they become soggy.

Store unfilled cannoli shells in an airtight container fitted with a paper towel (to absorb moisture) at room temperature for up to 7 days.

NOTE: *About 8 hours before you fill the cannoli, drain the ricotta. Line a colander with cheesecloth and place over a bowl. Spoon the ricotta into the colander. Cover and refrigerate for at least 8 hours or up to overnight. If the ricotta is not drained, the filling will be too watery and drip out of the ends of the stuffed cannoli shells.*

SOURCES FOR INGREDIENTS & EQUIPMENT

Many of these items are also available via Amazon.com and at stores in your area.

INGREDIENTS

ALTERNATIVE SUGARS

NOW FOODS / www.nowfoods.com
Including beet, palm, date, and maple.

ANISE OIL AND LEMON OIL

HOUSE ON THE HILL / www.houseonthehill.net
Also carries molds (see page 162).

FOOD COLORING

ATECO / www.atecousa.com
I use the gel food coloring line. A little goes a long way, and the colors are excellent.

GLUTEN-FREE FLOURS AND GUMS

BOB'S RED MILL / www.bobsredmill.com
Carries all the flours used in my mix, as well as xanthan gum. I do not recommend the company's gluten-free flour mix, which contains bean flour (and makes the mix taste beany) and lacks xanthan gum.

AUTHENTIC FOODS / www.authenticfoods.com
Sells all the flours used in my mix, as well as xanthan gum. The Multi Blend Flour is a mix that, of all those available on the market, performs closest to mine.

Other gluten-free flour mixes similar to mine are available from the following sources:

SIMPLY GLUTEN-FREE / www.simplygluten-free.com
Carol's All Purpose, Pastry Flour mix is close in performance to mine.

JULES GLUTEN-FREE / www.julesglutenfree.com
Jules Gluten Free All Purpose Flour.

BETTER BATTER / www.betterbatter.org
Better Batter All Purpose Flour Mix.

OIL

CALIFORNIA RICE BRAN OIL / www.californiariceoil.com
This is my favorite oil for frying and for use as a neutral-flavored oil in baking and cooking. I use it a lot and buy it in gallon containers.

SEA SALT

REAL SALT / www.realsalt.com
This is my favorite basic fine sea salt, which I use as my table and baking salt. This source also carries a kosher salt that I use for Chocolate Chip Cookies (page 60).

SPICES AND SEEDS

PENZEYS SPICES / www.penzeys.com
Especially anise seeds and saffron threads. Spices from Penzeys are the best available, and they are strong and flavorful, much more than the spices you get at the grocery store.

SUGAR SPRINKLES

INDIA TREE / www.indiatree.com
This site has a complete ingredients list for each product, including a handy allergen chart. Sparkling Sugar is the company's name for the sprinkles.

SUNFLOWER SEED BUTTER

SUNBUTTER / www.sunbutter.com
This is terrific on its own or as a peanut butter substitute. It is made in a factory that is peanut-free.

YEAST

RED STAR YEAST / www.redstaryeast.com
I like active dry yeast, instead of instant or fast-acting yeast or fresh cakes. I get Red Star yeast in 2-lb/910-g bags (I use a lot). Red Star yeast in small jars can be found at grocery stores. The amounts used in the recipes in this book require different measurements than the standard quantity in individual packets. So I don't recommend the packets if you have other options. It's not bad—just a hassle. If you do use the packets, note that 1 packet is equal to 2¼ tsp. Keep in mind that 1 Tbsp yeast is 3 tsp.

EQUIPMENT

BAKING PANS

WILLIAMS-SONOMA / www.williams-sonoma.com
The company has a terrific selection of heavy-duty metal baking pans that won't warp, rust, or corrode, and are not nonstick. I like the Traditional Finish line—the pans are made of aluminized steel and heat evenly. They are reasonably priced and dishwasher safe.

BUNDT PANS

NORDIC WARE / www.buynordicware.com
The company's Bundt pans are heavy-duty and long-lasting. Many shapes are available—I have several. Some shapes are particularly suited for holiday baking, including the Holiday Tree, Gingerbread House, and Star of David pans. You want a pan with a capacity of at least 9 or 10 cups/2.1 or 2.4 L, which will be appropriate for most Bundt cake recipes.

CANNOLI TUBES

ATECO / www.atecousa.net
The Ateco 660 Cannoli Kit comes with 4 reusable stainless-steel tubes.

COOKIE CUTTERS

ATECO / www.atecousa.net
The company has sets and individual cutters. I use the round cookie cutter set #5357 a lot for the recipes in this book. It has eleven stainless-steel cutters ranging from ¾ in/2 cm to 3½ in/9 cm diameter. I highly recommend this set.

FOX RUN / www.foxrunbrands.com
I like Fox Run's six-piece star cutter set (#3686) because the stars are more pointy and sharply defined than those made by other companies.

COOKIE PRESS

KUHN RIKON / www.kuhnrikon.com
The press comes with attachments for making cookies and tools for decorating.

COOKIE SHEETS AND HALF SHEET PANS

FOX RUN / www.foxrunbrands.com
Hands down, the absolute best cookie sheets and half sheet pans are made by Doughmakers. What makes these pans so good is that they are heavy-duty aluminum and have a pebbled surface that promotes even baking. The pebbled surface makes the pans a bit nonstick. I highly recommend the pans. They last forever. You will never need to buy another cookie sheet again.

KRUMKAKE AND PIZZELLE IRONS

CHEF'S CHOICE / www.edgecraft.com
I use the 839 Krumkake Express, a stand-alone, electric iron. My choice for *pizzelles* is the 835 Pizzelle Pro Express Bake, also a stand-alone, electric iron. There are also many choices of stove-top irons.

PANETTONE MOLDS

FANTES KITCHENWARE / www.fantes.com
The disposable molds that I use for baking panettone are the medium-sized, #17815, measuring 6 by 4 in/15 by 10 cm.

PARCHMENT PAPER

www.ifyoucare.com
This brand is unbleached and coated with silicon, and can be composted.

ROSETTE IRONS

FANTES KITCHENWARE / www.fantes.com
EBAY / www.ebay.com
There are many rosette irons on the market. The traditional shape is a rosette flower, but all sorts of shapes are available. The best irons are cast iron, yet are hard to find new. Vintage irons are often for sale on eBay. The next best alternative irons are cast aluminum, which are widely available.

SCALE

ESCALI / www.escali.com
I use the Primo Kitchen Scale, a nicely priced scale that measures in both grams and ounces.

SPRINGERLE AND SPECULAAS MOLDS

House on the Hill / www.houseonthehill.net
There are many other mold makers. I think this source offers one of the most comprehensive selections.

STEAMED PUDDING MOLD

FANTES KITCHENWARE / www.fantes.com
I use the #6773, a mold with a capacity of about 2 qt/2 L. It is in the traditional pudding shape.

TRIFLE BOWL

ANCHOR HOCKING / www.anchorhocking.com
There are many styles to choose from. The traditional one is a pedestal type; others do not have a stem.

INDEX